NICELY NURDLED, SIR

Christopher Lee

NICELY NURDLED, SIR!

New Enlarged Edition

BANTAM PRESS

LONDON · NEW YORK · TORONTO · SYDNEY · AUCKLAND

TRANSWORLD PUBLISHERS LTD
61–63 Uxbridge Road, London W5 5SA

TRANSWORLD PUBLISHERS (AUSTRALIA) PTY LTD
15–23 Helles Avenue, Moorebank, NSW 2170

TRANSWORLD PUBLISHERS (NZ) LTD
Cnr Moselle and Waipareira Aves,
Henderson, Auckland

Published 1988 by Bantam Press
a division of Transworld Publishers Ltd
Copyright © 1986, 1988 by Christopher Lee

First published 1986 by Elm Tree Books.
This revised and enlarged edition first
published by Bantam Press 1988.
This book is set in Garamond
by Goodfellow & Egan Ltd, Cambridge

British Library Cataloguing in Publication Data

Lee, Christopher, *1941*–
    Nicely nurdled, Sir.——New enl. ed.
    1. Cricket
    I. Title
    796.35′8

ISBN 0-593-01656-4

Printed in Great Britain by Biddles Ltd., Guildford and King's Lynn.

Contents

The Greatest Game   1

Flannelled Heroes   34

The Old Man and All   50

Funny, Not Out   67

The Nave that Took Spin   85

On Hallowed Ground   97

A Boys' Own Game   109

In Middle Meadow   125

A New Day   136

Close of Play   146

Sources and Acknowledgements   163

Reading List   169

To
Tiggy and Pom

The Greatest Game

Dozing in deckchair's gentle curve,
through half-closed eyes, I watched the cricket.

John Arlott

Anyone who has seen a good village cricketer nurdle one round to leg and all along the ground knows that special feeling. It is contentment. It is indeed a sight best seen through half-closed eyes, from the comfort of deckchair's gentle curve. It brings not a roar from some mounded stand, but merely a murmur of knowing approval from benches and rugs. It is a moment when eyes, hands, feet, balance and timing come together . . . not in some mighty loft over the ropes for six, nor in a dancer's delicate late cut for four. It is the one shot that, for a moment, is as good as any played by the greatest in the greatest game of them all.

1

MITCHAM GREEN

Sussex were playing Surrey. The afternoon sun was warm, the breeze gentle and the grass still sweet and soft. Sitting there was a silver-haired old gentleman whose playing days were clearly over but who had, apparently, been something of a wicket-keeper. Every so often he would nod off ... it had been a good lunch. Sussex were batting, and it was Greig who picked a ball off his pads and delicately turned it down to the fine leg boundary. The old fellow stirred gently and muttered, 'Nicely nurdled, sir! Nicely nurdled.' And with a contented smile he nodded off once more.

It was a perfect afternoon. Perhaps that's what cricket is, a perfect afternoon. A game of chosen memories. Were not the great players manly, clean-cut and cream-flannelled? Illusions perhaps, but why not? Cricket after all is not simply a game. Cricket is The Game.

They'll tell you it all started in Hambledon. They'd be wrong. Some say the monks played at 'crekkits' in the fourteenth century. Maybe. But they did play at the Royal Grammar School at Guildford in about 1550. In the record of the Court Leet it is noted that one John Derrick, 'being a scholler in the free Schools of Guldeford hee and divers of his fellowes did runne and play there at Creckett and other Plaies ....' And the seventeenth-century parson, Thomas Wilson, a pious man, appeared to accept cricket as an everyday event:

> Maidstone was formerly a very prophane town, insomuch that I have seen morris-dancing, cudgel-playing, stool-ball, crickets and many other sports openly and publikly on the Lord's day.

3

On the Sabbath indeed! In truth, the Anglican clergy have always had close connections with cricket. More than three hundred years ago one of them, Henry Teonge, was a chaplain aboard His Majesty's Ship *Royal Oak*, somewhere in the eastern Mediterranean.

> On May 6, 1676 this morning early, at least forty of the English, with his worship the Consull, rode out of the cytty about four miles to the Greene Platt, a fine vally by the river syde; to recreate themselves, where a princely tent was pitched: and we had severall pastimes and sports, as duck-hunting, fishing, shooting, hand-ball, Krickett, scrofilo: and then a noble dinner brought thither with greate plenty of all sorts of wines, punch, and lemonade and at six wee returned all home in good order, but soundly tyred and weary.

Sounds much like any other village game. Thirty years later cricket was being advertised in the south-east of England as a team game. Newspapers carried reports. In 1705 a Kent paper recorded that eleven gentlemen of the west part of the county had played eleven of Chatham for eleven guineas a man. In fine white silk stockings and blue breeches, it had become the sport of publicans, gamekeepers, baronets and dukes. Richard Hayes, the diarist and an eighteenth-century cricket enthusiast, noted in June 1776 a special game in Kent:

> I set off about seven in the morning to Seven-oaks Vine to see Hambledon play with All England at cricket. The Duke of Dorset bowled out after getting about six runs. I heard him say if he missed a ball he was sure

4

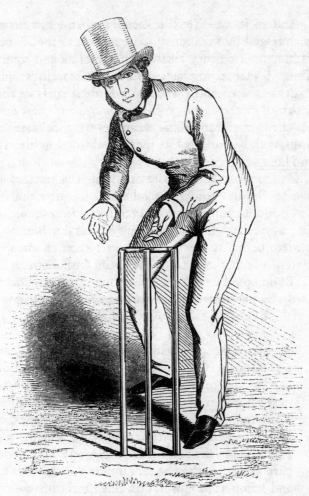

TOM BOX OF SUSSEX

to be out. The Hambledon men were in between five and six hours. They beat us in guarding their wickets and in standing out too. NB They talk of having three stumps. By their playing with very broad bats and playing all the blocking short play, it is very hard matter to hit a wicket.

5

And so it was. Yet the keenness of the game was encouraged by the money to be made and the chance of fame in a century taken with gambling and sometimes brutal enjoyment. Bloodied stockings and knuckles bared and gashed played their parts in this sport of wagers and rivalry. Dukes and baronets poached gamekeepers and wagoners who had reputations with ball and bat as they would buy huntsmen and bold Irish mares.

One patron, both sportsman and cricketer, was Squire Osbaldeston. Here he writes about Lambert and Budd. Lambert came from Surrey where they said he was one of the finest strikers of ball, bowlers and fielders of his time. They said in Sussex, Kent and Hampshire that this might have been true. Though E. H. Budd could have been the stronger batsman, with hard straight arms and hands that seemed ever gripped. Osbaldeston played with them both:

As wicket-keeper, fieldsman, bowler and batter, no man ever equalled Lambert. Apropos batting and catching, Mr Budd was the hardest hitter I ever saw; several times he hit the ball over the palings without touching them. In one match Lambert was bowling and Mr Budd caught the ball a half-volley, hitting it as hard as he did when he sent it over the palings, and Lambert caught it with one hand, throwing it up as if he had taken it out of his pocket. The eye could only follow the ball for half a second and then it was out of sight.

Lambert was the first to discover I was so fast a bowler. Lord Frederick Beauclerc, a first-rate player, very long-headed and a great judge of the game, was not then aware that I could bowl so great a pace, and by the advice of Lambert I made a match to play against Lord Frederick and Howard; the latter not so fast a bowler as I was, but steadier. Some time before the match came off I was taken very ill and was confined to my room. I wrote to Lord Frederick, informing him of my situation and saying how obliged I should be to him if he would consent to postpone the match. He wrote a very laconic answer back, declining my request, and I thought nothing then remained to be settled but a forfeit. I named this to Lambert, who came to see me. He said, 'I think if I could be allowed a fieldsman I could beat them both.' I told him I thought such an issue never could occur, but if he liked to try the experiment he should have the stakes if he won.

I applied for a fieldsman, but with the same result as attended my suggestion of postponement. Lambert then said that if I could only hit a ball and get a run he could claim a fieldsman. I told him I was so weak and reduced I could never accomplish it; but at his earnest desire I consented and went to Lord's in my carriage. Fully half the match was over and Lambert being just then out, I went in; but from the quantity of medicine I had taken, and being shockingly weak from long confinement to my room, I felt quite dizzy and faint. Lord Frederick bowled to me; luckily he was a slow bowler, and I could manage to get out of harm's way if necessary, but it did not so happen. I hit one of his balls so hard I had time to walk a run. He then became vexed and desired Howard (Lord Frederick's partner) to bowl; but I gave up my bat and claimed a fieldsman. This claim was not admitted. When I walked the run many of the spectators cheered, all the cricketers knowing the circumstances. The match was not over that day as Lord Frederick had to go in against Lambert's score. I attended and saw the issue, and was never more gratified in my life than I was when Lambert bowled his Lordship out and won the match.

And Budd it was who breaks the spell of jolly yeomen simply having a good time while all about them is ever green, soft mown grass and the froth of hops and malt. As his conversation with the Reverend James Pycroft suggests (yet no confessor he), the bets and exchange of promises were never far from notcher's stick and mark:

'In 1817, we went,' said Mr Budd, 'with Osbaldston to play twenty-two of Nottingham. In that match Clarke played. In common with others, I lost my money, and was greatly disappointed at the termination. One paid player was accused of selling, and never employed after. The concourse of people was very great: these were the days of the Luddites (rioters), and the magistrates warned us, that unless we would stop our game at seven o'clock, they could not answer for keeping the peace. At seven o'clock we stopped; and, simultaneously, the thousands who lined the ground began to close in upon us. Lord Frederick lost nerve and was very much alarmed; but I said they didn't want to hurt us. No; they simply came to have a look at the eleven men who ventured to play two for one.'

8

Lord Frederick was one of a line of noble batters in a game that captured the imagination of royalty itself. In 1737, Frederick, the Prince of Wales, took part in a right royal and ducal affair, with nearly very sad results, as the *Evening Post* noted:

> The great cricket match between HRH the Prince of Wales for Surrey and London and Lord John Sackville, son of His Grace, the Duke of Dorset for Kent, was played on Kennington Common . . . the press was so great on the occasion that a poor woman, by the crowd bearing upon her, unfortunately had her leg broke, which being related to His Royal Highness, he was placed to order her ten guineas.

Might his generosity have been rewarded in another place far from average mongering? For HRH must have been one of the first recorded fatal victims of The Game, as recorded in Wraxall's memoirs:

> Frederick, Prince of Wales, son of George II, expired suddenly in 1751, at Leicester House, in the arms of Desnoyers, the celebrated dancing master. His end was caused by an internal abscess that had long been forming in consequence of a blow which he received in the side from a cricket ball while he was engaged in playing at the game on the lawn at Cliefden House in Buckinghamshire, where he then principally resided. Death did not take place, however, till several months after the accident, when a collection of matter burst and instantly suffocated him.

GREENWICH PENSIONERS' CRICKET MATCH, AT THE PRIORY GROUNDS, NEAR LEWISHAM

Cricket may have always been a dangerous game - how much more so in its more macabre moments. In 1848, a Mr Ingersoll of Lewisham, which was not far from the Greenwich Naval Hospital, put together an almost grotesque match. He set up a game between a team of one-legged sailors to play one-armed sailors. Furthermore, it was a two-day game. This is the match report carried in the *London Illustrated News* of Saturday, 9 September 1848, together with an equally grotesque illustration of the event:

By the kind permission of the authorities of Greenwich Hospital, the hardy veterans of that splendid establishment were entertained at a cricket match on Monday and Tuesday, in the Priory grounds, near Lewisham. The novelty of the conditions upon which alone these worn-out sons of the ocean would be allowed to enter the lists, was the cause of a large and fashionable party attending each day. These conditions were, that twenty-two men should be chosen for the field, one half of whom should be minus an arm, and the other a leg! Yet there was no lack of candidates for the honours of the bat and ball, and the number was very soon selected. The weather, too, was beautifully fine; the locality selected for the display a most charming spot; and the spectators as well as the actors appeared to be highly amused.

A large tent had been erected on the southern side of the field, and within it was spread forth an ample supply of the creature comforts of this life, to which the dilapidated tars did ample justice. They were invited to this entertainment by Mr Ingersoll, of

11

Lewisham, who, in conjunction with Mr Ireland and Mr Staunton, had got it up at their sole expence, in addition to distributing a sum of money amongst the competitors. Upon the first day the wickets were pitched, and the sports commenced shortly after two o'clock, the bands striking up 'Rule Britannia', the eleven one-armed men taking the first innings; and during the whole time the bats and balls were at work, the spectators were kept in an almost continuous roar of laughter by the grotesque figures the poor old veterans made as they measured their length on the slippery sward in their vain efforts to reach the ball, or to exercise their diminished 'under-standing' beyond their ordinary gait to reach the goal in time.

Upon the first day the one-arms made 50 runs in the first start, and 41 at the second. On Tuesday they assembled again with renewed vigour; and now the wooden legs went at it in high glee. Their first innings made 32, and their second 43; thus leaving the game to the one-arms by 16. Nothing could exceed the delight with which they appeared to enjoy the sport, or the kindness and courteous attention of Mr Ingersoll to all their wants. The game was concluded by six o'clock; and then the hardy old blue-coats marched in procession from the ground, headed by the band, banners, etc., and were again entertained at a party feast by Mr Ingersoll, at the Black Bull Inn.

Lord Frederick Beauclerc himself had declared that the game was for men, indeed scar and limp were badges and insignia of the sport. When shown the first set of pads, or leggings as they were called, he declared they would never be used because they were unfair. Under the trousers they had to go, hidden lest cowardice were called.

Alfred Mynn, the mighty round-arm bowler from Kent, learned the hard way. He was playing at Leicester, more known at the time for a different form of leather hunting (this in 1836). A ball from one Samuel Redgate struck Mynn on his unguarded legs. Down he went. Down he stayed. Then splints were called and a makeshift bed. The groaning demon was wedged atop a London stage-coach. At St Bartholomew's Hospital they cried, 'Off with his leg.' Thank, though, the gods of cricket for second opinions. Cold compresses for two years and he was back - this time, it is said, with leggings.

But let not the knocks, welts and fractures of this play of gentlemen and others hide the skills of even the most casual and agricultural players - especially those in the late eighteenth and early nineteenth centuries. Richard Hayes had noted the difficulty of hitting two stumps spread apart in dorian simplicity. A year earlier, in 1775 John Nyren had watched Lumpy Stevens foxing the batsmen's reach and stroke, only to be cheated by more than the hair's breadth that lay between stump and stump:

> On the 22nd of May 1775, a match was played in the artillery Ground, between five of the Hambledon Club and five of All England; when Small went in the last man for fourteen runs and fetched them. Lumpy was bowler on the occasion; and it having been remarked that his balls had several times passed between Small's stumps, it was considered to be hard

13

thing upon the bowler that his straightest balls should have been thus sacrificed; the number of the stumps was in consequence increased from two to three.

But not everywhere. The news travelled slowly and others were reluctant to give way, especially if the patrons were batsmen. Yet this notice from the *Kentish Gazette* of 4 June 1777 appears convincing evidence that the days when batsmen had it their own way were indeed numbered:

> On Sevenoaks Vine on Wednesday 18th June instant will be played the first match for a thousand guineas. Hampshire against All England. The wicket to be pitched at ten o'clock and to be played with three stumps to shorten the game.

And so with stuttering side-steps gathering to generous speed, the under-arm hurlers of the eighteenth century whizzed and fizzed their way towards more wickets and the enjoyed frustrations of many of their masters, most of whom fancied themselves as batsmen. (Might the Warden have sat on sheltered bench and wondered why Gentleman whipped and scourged the bowling of servant? Why brother called for sister to bowl to him? Why night nursery dreamed of cuts, drives and glances while scullery bred guile of lob, pitch and turn? He might.)

A hundred years, or nearly, passed, and bowlers worried still. And so in Lancashire, in 1872, there came a game between Manchester and Birkenhead Park, with not three but four stumps pressed in the drizzled turf. Yet it made little difference. As G. T.

Knight had remarked, years earlier, there was more to bowling than three sticks and four:

> The object is not to bring the batting down to the bowling in order to equalize them, but to exalt the latter to the level of the former; not to diminish the means of defence, but to add to the powers of the attack. A wicket may be extended to the size of a gate, or a bat diminished to that of a walking-stick; and at some intermediate point, there is no doubt but that men may be got out with tolerable certainty, just as a log of sufficient weight will reduce the speed of a racehorse to that of a pig.

A year earlier, Knight had played in an important trial of styles. There had been considerable anger at the idea that bowlers might move from under-arm to round-arm. A three-match trial between Sussex and All England was fixed to test the caddish round-arm bowling. The old style of under-arm had been conquered by the batsmen and many of them viewed the modern method, which they regarded as throwing, with considerable alarm. In fact, in 1827, a group of the All England players threatened to pull out of the game with Sussex because the southern side bowled the new and 'unfair' way:

> We the undersigned do agree, that we will not play the third match between All England and Sussex, which is intended to be at Brighton, in July or August, unless the Sussex players bowl fair; that is, abstain from THROWING. T. Marsden, W. Ashby, W. Matthews, W. Searle, J.

Saunders, T. C. Howard, W. Caldecourt, F. Pilch, T. Beagley.

But play they did. Yet it was not until 1864 that the bowler was allowed to turn his arm over, rather than under or round. Throwing, some said. Disgraceful, said others. At least noteworthy, as the Honourable R. H. Lyttleton remarked in a review of the century:

> Since 1827 the only noteworthy revolution which has taken place was in 1864, when the bowler was allowed to deliver the ball with his arm above the shoulder, a most important concession, only granted at the time after fierce opposition. The bowling of Spofforth at his fastest, Ulyett, Mr Rotherham and others on the old-fashioned wickets, before the introduction of the mowing-machine and heavy roller, would have prevented heavy run-getting by the simple expedient of severely injuring the batsman – not a desirable method by any means. But the new rule for a time somewhat diminished scores, and only ceased to be more efficacious as the grounds improved. As far as bowling is concerned things have not altered since, and it is impossible that any further change can take place, as public opinion has spoken out strongly in regard to throwing, which owing to the weakness of umpires and the great laxity of cricket committees crept into vogue a few years ago.

For some, ten stumps could be set up and it would still be a very hard matter. But what is cricket? I remember my schoolmaster, stooped and waistcoated still though it was late June, reading precious lines. It

was, he droned, a manly, true and chivalrous sport. Rudyard Kipling was a little more down-to-earth. He said it was casting a ball at three straight sticks and defending the same with a fourth. Charles Box, with a certain Victorian flair, said maybe, but it was all part of the Englishness of The Game:

> In no other country but England would the attack and defence of three stumps be witnessed by enormous crowds of fashionable people with unflagging zest, and there are not many foreigners as yet who would care to face a swift bowler with no more protection than a bat.

Cricket is certainly a fashionable game, although only among fashionable people, as P. G. Wodehouse pointed out in *Piccadilly Jim*: 'Oh, I am glad you have begun to take an interest in cricket. It is simply a social necessity in England. . . . ' Wodehouse was a very agreeable man. William Hazlitt, the essayist, was sometimes very disagreeable. But he knew all about cricket and the effects on the early Victorians: 'The very names of cricket bat and ball make English fingers tingle. . . . '

Now why should fingers tingle? Long summer afternoons? Home-county sandwiches on soft rugs? Worcester's tall spire? The first close cut of new grass? Perhaps it's anticipation of warm sun after a long winter and a damp spring. H. S. Vere Hodge knew. He played his cricket in Essex and, with his pen, sketched and scanned the greatest game:

Chant Royal of Cricket

When earth awakes as from some dreadful night
   And doffs her melancholy mourning state,
When May buds burst in blossom and requite
   Our weary eyes for Winter's tedious wait,
Then the pale bard takes down his dusty lyre
   And strikes the thing with more than usual fire.
Myself, compacted of an earthier clay,
   I oil my bats and greasy homage pay
To Cricket, who, with emblems of his court,
   Stumps, pads, bails, gloves, begins his summer
      sway.
Cricket in sooth is Sovran King of Sport.

As yet no shadows blue the magic light,
   The glamour that surrounds the opening date.
Illusions yet undashed my soul excite
   And of success in luring whispers prate.
I see myself in form: my thoughts aspire
   To reach the giddy summit of desire.
Lovers and such may sing a roundelay,
   Whate'er that be, to greet returning May:
For me, not much – the season's all too short:
   I hear the mower hum and scent the fray.
Cricket in sooth is Sovran King of Sport.

A picture stands before my dazzled sight,
   Wherein the hero, ruthlessly elate,
Defies all bowlers' concentrated spite.
   That hero is myself, I need not state.
'Tis sweet to see the captain's growing ire
   And his relief when I at last retire;
'Tis sweet to run pavilionwards and say,
   'Yes, somehow I WAS seeing them today' –

19

Thus modesty demands that I retort
    To murmured compliments upon my play.
Cricket in sooth is Sovran King of Sport.

The truth's resemblance is, I own, but slight
    To these proud visions which my soul inflate.
This is the sort of thing: in abject fright
    I totter down the steps and through the gate;
Somehow I reach the pitch and bleat, 'Umpire,
    Is that one leg?' What boots it to enquire?
The impatient bowler takes one grim survey,
    Speeds to the crease and whirls – a lightning ray?
No, a fast yorker. Bang! the stumps cavort.
    Chastened, but not surprised, I go my way.
Cricket in sooth is Sovran King of Sport.

Lord of the Game, for whom these lines I write,
    Fulfil my present hope, watch o'er my fate;
Defend me from the swerver's puzzling flight;
    Let me not be run out, at any rate.
As one who's been for years a constant trier,
    Reward me with an average slightly higher;
Let it be double figures. This I pray,
    Humblest of boons, before my hair grows grey
And Time's flight bids me in the last resort
    Try golf, or otherwise your cause betray.
Cricket in sooth is Sovran King of Sport.

King, what through Age's summons I obey
    Resigned to dull rheumatics and decay,
Still on one text my hearers I'll exhort,
    As long as hearers within range will stay,
'Cricket in sooth is Sovran King of Sport.'

So there we have the hope that comes in May when
a young man's fancy turns also to cricket. Old
Andrew Lang learned his cricket in the Scottish

border country, in the middle of the last century:

The first time I ever saw bat and ball must have been about 1850. The gardener's boy and his friends were playing with home-made bats, made out of firwood with the bark on, and with a gutta-percha ball. The game instantly fascinated me, and when I once understood why the players ran after making a hit, the essential difficulties of comprehension were overcome. Already the border towns, Hawick, Kelso, Selkirk, Galashiels, had their elevens. To a small boy the spectacle of the various red and blue caps and shirts was very delightful. The grounds were, as a rule, very rough and bad. Generally the play was on haughs, level pieces of town-land beside the rivers. Then the manufacturers would encroach on the cricket-field, and build a mill on it, and cricket would have to seek new settlements.

In these early days, when one was only a small spectator, ay, and in later days too, the great difficulty of cricket was that excellent thing in itself, too much patriotism. Almost the whole population of a town would come to the ground and take such a keen interest in the fortunes of their side, that the other side, if it won, was in some danger of rough handling. Probably no one was ever much hurt; indeed, the squabbles were rather a sham fight than otherwise; but still, bad feeling was caused by umpires' decisions. Then relations would be broken off between the clubs of different towns, and sometimes this tedious hostility endured for years.

THE ROYAL FAMILY IN THE HIGHLANDS: CRICKET MATCH AT BALMORAL; BALMORAL AGAINST ABERGELDIE

Later, in the same article, Lang wrote:

Our wickets keep falling in this life. One after the other goes down. They are becoming few who joined in those Border matches where there was but one lazy spectator, when we made such infrequent runs, and often dropped a catch, but never lost heart, never lost pleasure in the game. Some of them may read this, and remember old friends gone, old games played, old pewters drained, old pipes smoked, old stories told, remember the leg-hitting of Jack Grey, the bowling of Bill Dryden and of Clement Glassford, the sturdy defence of William Forman. And he who writes, recalling that simple delight and good fellowship, recalling those kind faces and merry days in the land of Walter Scott, may make his confession, and may say that such years were worth living for, and that neither study, nor praise, nor any other pleasure has equalled, or can equal, the joy of having been young and a cricketer. . . .

To Lang cricket was more than a game. He believed that there is no talk, none so witty and brilliant, that is as good as cricket talk, when memory sharpens memory and the dead live again:

Cricket is simply the most catholic and diffused, the most innocent, kindly and manly of popular pleasures, while it has been the delight of statesmen and the relaxation of learning.

It is also a game of miserable disappointment. As

Run out.

24

the essayist E. V. Lucas observed in the thirties, there is no second chance . . . Who would be a batsman out to bad chance? The man out first ball must retire to the pavilion and brood on his ill-luck until it is time to field and forget it – when, as likely as not, he will miss a catch and enter purgatory again. Still, as Lucas said, the cricketing temperament, always slightly sardonic, accepts it. He noted also that none of this applies to the poor cricketer:

> There is no other game at which the con-firmed duffer is so persistent and so unde-pressed. It is for the experts, victims of misfortune, that depression awaits; it is they who chew the cud of bitterness.

Mary Russell Mitford, writing of early nineteenth-century village life in Hampshire, was quite certain that if nothing else, cricket and industry went together:

> Note that your good cricketer is commonly the most industrious man in the parish; the habits that make him such are precisely those which make a good workman – steadiness, sobriety, and activity.

Sturdy stuff. Rule Britannia! Britannia rules the green sward. Very English. Hubert Phillips put it perfectly in one line: 'An Englishman's crease is 'is castle. . . . ' There's something very noble in that line. It's a reflection of the sentiments of an age gone by, perhaps. It doesn't quite tell of the back-street test matches where a black pit wall is the only wicket-keeper. So beware cant, as Neville Cardus reminds us:

The Victorians so endowed the game with their own moral grandeur that to this day the president of Little Puddleton cricket club cannot take the chair at the annual general meeting without telling his audience that criket is 'synonymous' with straight conduct, honour bright, and all the other recognized Christian virtues. Hear him: ' . . . on and off the field you must play the game. Cricket stands for all that is finest in the character of an Englishman. When we wish to say that something has been done that is not "true blue", we say, "It's not cricket." ' And so on and so forth, year after year. The wonder is that players of other games do not despise cricketers as so many prigs. This perpetual insistence on the 'gentlemanliness' of cricket seems to me as unnecessary as it is offensive. The Victorian wear of morality has been so well rubbed by long usage that it affects my imagination like a shabby clerical garment. If a fieldsman having held a ball sharply in the slips, after it has hit the ground – if he announces that the catch was not fair, the commentators are bound to say, 'Ah, there's cricket for you!' Not long ago Richard Tyldesley of Lancashire held a ball in this way, and he immediately told the batsman to remain at the crease. In my report of the match I humorously applauded Tyldesley's action, adding that it did credit to Westhoughton Sunday School. But innumerable correspondents wrote taking me to task for attempting to be 'funny' over an act of 'real cricket'. Why should a cricketer be especially singled out for moral approbation because he plays according to the rules? And why when footballers and jockeys 'play the game', why are they not applauded likewise, and their games exalted to the realms of ethical? There is little or no betting in modern cricket, true. But there was any amount of betting on cricket matches a hundred years ago. The long-drawn-out character of a modern first-class cricket match does not favour the gambling instincts; they are better suited by quicker sports and pastimes. That, I fancy, is the main reason why cricket is 'clean' – not because cricketers are as a class more pure in heart than any other sportsmen. Moral superiority is the worst form of priggishness; for that reason I hate the false view of chivalry which in recent years has belittled more than one cricket match.

Surely Mr Cardus would not really wish to wipe away our illusions about the Englishness of cricket, would he? Certainly he believed that cricket could be a great leveller:

A true batsman should in most of his strokes tell the truth about himself. An innings by Lord Aberdare comes straight out of Debrett's. And an innings by Richard Tyldesley comes straight out of Westhoughton. The accent in each case is true. If Tyldesley were to flash his leg over to the off and drive a ball through the covers with Lord Aberdare's aristocratic pose it would be as false as if the man himself came to me and said, 'I beg to differ from you on certain equivocal points in your critique of my play this morning.' And if Lord Aberdare were to clout a ball high and hard, using Tyldesley's comically cross bat, it would be equally false – as though he were to say to me, 'Tha'rt a nice soart to talk about t'game. Ah'd like to bowl at thee!'

This difference in perception is summed up, neatly of course, by J. B. Priestley in *The English*. It is not a matter of caste but of understanding; knowing when the common bond of cricket is at best a keen competition and at worst a battlefield. How we play the game tells us something about ourselves, as Mr Cardus pointed out. J. B. Priestley understood that the underlying attraction of the game is the suggestion that there is time to be there, to watch or to play. Time is for once on all sides:

In spite of recent jazzed-up matches, cricket to be fully appreciated demands leisure, some sunny warm days, and an understanding of its finer points – and it depends more than any other ball game on varying conditions, on the state of the pitch, on weather and wind and light, it multiplies its fine points. Though it is often considered a 'gentlemanly game', an idea supported by its leisurely progress and breaks for lunch, tea, cool drinks on the field, we must remember that many of its greatest performers came from the Industrial North, which also supplied, until our own time, large numbers of its most knowledgeable and keenest spectators.

Like regiments of the British army, geography only suggests but cannot prescribe the claims of cricket on British life. One hundred and fifty years after Lumpy Stevens and Small and Budd and Lambert were in their prime, that venerable institution the British Council published a series of essays to show foreigners what the British were about. The essays included one on cricket and what it meant to us all. As we were being beaten on a regular basis, certainly by the Australians, some might have thought this intelligence well known:

> Almost every other game of sport with which we entertain ourselves belongs also today to many other countries, but cricket, that defence of two citadels of three stumps apiece against the missile of a ball, has never taken root anywhere save in English-speaking countries, and so it is our most typically national game. . . .
> The stranger is apt to make his first aquaintance with cricket at a big match, possibly at Lord's ground in London. . . . It is certain that he will hear with some amazement that this match occupies three days. He will wonder how there are so many people who can afford to be idle, and secondly how they can be satisfied for long spells of time with so little action.
> Surely he will think they must be held there by some singular magic and he had best accept that view until he has watched for some little while and come to feel the spell himself. Fascinating it must be, for once the spectator has settled down in the sunshine, he is most unwilling to go away. He declares virtuously that he must go, that he will stay only another five minutes, ten minutes, quarter of an hour. The big clock ticks out those minutes relentlessly; there is no pretence that he cannot see

29

it, and still he remains as the day wears on and the shadows of the players grow longer. There is always some temptation to remain, to see if a batsman reaches a particular score or, should he depart, to see how his successor will fare. And cricket is essentially a sunshine game. In its nature it cannot be played in time of tempest. Like a sundial it only counts the sunny hours and as soon as the raindrops fall the white figures vanish . . .

Far from Mr Cardus's warnings against cant and its pits and traps.

Rudyard Kipling knew also the cant and humbug of those who would tell us to play up and play the game. Those same people might have expected us to find comfort in cricketing cries as our fathers and grandfathers slogged through some dreadful and dry playing field against rifle and bible and boer and, later, crouched in trenches in once beautiful France:

And ye sent them comfits and pictures to
    help them harry your foes
And ye vaunted your fathomless power, and ye
    flaunted your iron pride,
Ere ye fawned on the Younger Nations for the men
    who could shoot and ride!
Then ye returned to your trinkets;
    then ye countented your souls
With the flannelled fools at the wicket
    or the muddied oafs at the goals.
Given to strong delusion, wholly believing
    a lie,
Ye saw that the land lay fenceless, and ye
    let the months go by

Waiting some easy wonder, hoping some saving
     sign –
  Idle – openly idle – in the lee of the fore-
spent line.
  Idle – except for your boasting – and what is
     your
boasting worth
  If ye grudge a year of service to the lordliest
life on earth?
  Ancient, effortless, ordered, cycle on
cycle set,
  Life so long untroubled, that ye who inherit
forget
  It was not made with the mountains, it is not
one with the deep.
  Men, not gods, devised it. Men, not gods, must
     keep.
Men, not children, servants, or kinsfolk called
     from afar,
But each man born in the Island broke to the
     matter of war,
Soberly and by custom taken and trained for
     the same,
Each man born in the Island entered at youth
     to the Game –
As it were almost cricket, not to be mastered in
     haste,
  But after trial and labour, by temperance,
living chaste.
  As it were almost cricket – as it were even
your play,
  Weighed and pondered and worshipped, and
practised day and day.

So is The Game and its sentiment an illusion? Why
sing in verse and hymn in praise of this famous game?

Is it only flannelled fools who choose their memories?
Like Edmund Blunden's labourer, dreaming of bat
and ball:

The Season Opens

'A tower we must have, and a clock in the tower,
  Looking over the tombs, the tithebarn, the
      bower;
The inn and the mill, the forge and the ball.'

So a grey tower we have, and centuried trees
  Have arisen to share what its belfry-light sees,
The apple-plats richest in spring-song of all,
  Kitchen gardens and the field where they take
bat and ball.

The stream with its movements of dance in the sun
  Where the willow allow, runs and ever will run
At the cleft of the orchard, along the soft fall
  Of the pasture where tourneys become bat and
ball.

And now where the confident cuckoo takes flight
  Over buttercups kindled in millions last night,

A labourer leans on the stackyard's low wall
    With the hens bothering round him, and dreams
bat and ball.

Till the meadow is quick with the masters who
        were
    And he hears his own shouts when he first
        trotted there;
Long ago; all gone home now; but here they come
        all!
    Surely these are the same, who now bring bat and
        ball?

GUNN CUTTING

Flannelled Heroes

The year was 1947. A small, sturdy lad in grey, scratchy short trousers and pocket-torn school blazer stared into the window of Mr Dorman's village shop. The season had drawn to a glorious end. And there in this window was a picture of my hero, D. C. S. Compton. Beside the smiling picture of the Brylcreamed record setter – eighteen centuries that year – was The Bat. A real three-springer it was. A white smooth blade with two words written across at an angle. The Driver. The lad eyed the name and the red rubber-covered handle with the proper silent seriousness of a seven-year-old. 'The Driver.' He mouthed the words carefully and with great awe. Then glumly he re-read the small piece of postcard upon which was written 'BAT ELEVEN SHILLINGS'. Eleven shillings! Not even at Christmas had he ever seen eleven shillings. he didn't know anyone who had. And then one morning, on the way to school, he saw the empty window.

'Sold,' said Mr Dorman.

The misery! And the picture of Compton?

'Gone,' said Mr Dorman.

Adults can be very cruel when they hide their joy. The misery continued right until Christmas morning. The Driver, the real three-springer with the red handle, appeared at the foot of his bed and under the

'The demon bowler.'

35

tree, the picture. Throughout the long winter, the passage between front door and kitchen became Lord's, the Oval, Old Trafford. Every day he was D. C. S. Compton. Another four to the dining-room door, a six into the dog's basket.

An ordinary tale? No, for cricket heroes are longer lasting than other sportsmen. But what makes a great cricketer? R. C. Robertson-Glasgow was an elegant player who became an even more elegant writer. He remembered Compton as a very young man:

> The first time that I saw Dennis Compton was in the nets at Lord's. He was bowling slow left-hand to an elderly member who wore a wildly improbable cap. Both performers were in a state of amusement and heat. Exercise rather than practice was being obtained . . . there was an abandon about the scene that cannot be forgotten; a copious enjoyment. . . . Enjoyment, given and felt, is the chief thing about Compton's batting. It has an ease and freshness which the formality of the first-class game has not injured. It is a clear flowing stream; a breath of half-holidays among work-days . . . nature and environment have been very good to him. Set fair to greatness.

'Set fair to greatness.' The same might have been said of Jack Hobbs, who was eighty-one when he died in 1963. John Arlott called him a modest, gentle, kindly man with a streak of flawless steel which he revealed only when honour demanded it:

> Jack Hobbs – Sir John Berry Hobbs – was the poor man's son who became the finest bats-man in the world, earned a knighthood, and

bore it with innate modesty and dignity. His ability with a cricket bat was such that the title of 'The Master' settled upon him as the recognition of the fact. He liked, though, to be known as 'Jack' and, if he had not been a famous sportsman, his personal qualities would still have made him outstanding within the circle of his acquaintance. He played a considerable part, too, in lifting the standing of his profession. To say that his knighthood was bestowed for batting does him less than justice. Nothing in his career is more significant than the fact that he was the first professional games player to be thus honoured. No one came nearer to defining the quality of his batting than Sir Pelham Warner when he said, 'Jack Hobbs is a professional who bats exactly like an amateur.'

The highest accolade indeed. He played like an amateur. A gentleman, not a professional. The supreme gentleman was that supreme amateur, K. S. Ranjitsinhji, The Maharaja Jamsahib of Nawanagar. They called him Ranji. He played for Sussex in the 1890s and early 1900s. His picture is in the library at the Hove ground and shows a slim, sensitive figure with a soft white shirt buttoned at the throat and wrist. Hugh de Selincourt, himself a Sussex man, saw him as an almost apologetic figure:

The Prince emerged slight and frail from the pavilion, his silk shirt buttoned round his wrist, fluttering on his arms: something in his manner suggested that it was rather a long walk to be expected to take on a hot day from the little gate to the wicket: still he took it

RANJI

with the best imaginable grace, carried his bat
too himself, and even consented to wear those
ungainly leg-shields known as pads. Before he
became their darling so that they would cheer
him if he removed his sweater, this noncha-
lance displeased people. I have heard him
hooted in an unimportant game at Lord's for
the way he chased after a ball at deep mid-
wicket; it was so against his nature to hurry or
take effort that he never seemed to run, but
most apologetically as it were to insinuate
himself over the ground. He smiled on that
occasion and saved the boundary. In later
years I have seen him field at point: he would
lazily step out and stop the hardest square-
cut, which most men would not have reached
with a jumping scramble, and lob lazily back
to the bowler. His batting had the same
appearance of effortlessness or rather perhaps
of an intense dislike of effort. You felt he
vastly preferred a fast bowler: indeed, was
generally grateful to him for the kind help of
his swift pace – the swifter, the kinder – in
sparing him the necessity of doing more than
tap the ball with quick wrist to long leg or cut
it through the slips. I saw him batting against
C. J. Kortright. It was cruel: it was pathetic.
The ball went to the boundary wherever the
three slips or long-leg continually shifted were
not. And if the bowler in despair pitched one
too far up, it was driven with sudden panther-
like fury between mid-off and extra-cover. It
seemed a waste of time to bother much about
the placing of the field: he always found a gap
and the gap always seemed to be the easiest
place for the shot, as though it had been

kindly left for his benefit. You felt in him the wish to apologise for clumsiness if he could chance to hit the ball within a fieldman's reach, after he had begun to feel in the least at home in his innings.

The lad now a man once stood in the upstairs room at the county ground in Hove. In his hands the green, slightly creased blazer that Ranji wore with its coarse hessian lining. Just think, Ranji's blazer. But what of Oldroyd's blazer? Oldroyd? In Yorkshire they'll tell you about Oldroyd, the antithesis of Ranji. A hard man, a man with a temper and a firey bat who never played for England. Robertson-Glasgow knew him:

His name might have been Jess Oakroyd. I'm not sure that it oughtn't to have been. For, as a cricketer, he was a type rather than an individual. He was one of those small, tough, humorous, militant men who make the comedy and the greatness of a country. They are to be found answering back something or somebody which may or may not have existence: fate, a tax-collector, Monday morning: a bus-conductor, thirst, a Hyde Park orator. They bounce and argue down time's corridors. And they generally win the battle. Oldroyd could not be one of those who, when they are abruptly bowled by a snorter, accept the unwelcome visitation with resigned calm. He was very angry indeed; and he looked it, and often said it. For you had not only ended Oldroyd for some hours; you'd ended an integral section of Yorkshire. You'd wrecked a parish and interfered with the workings of the only county that mattered. And there lies

40

the secret of the Yorkshire cricketer. He comes second in his own estimation; and he despises, if silently, those who cannot play to his philosophy.

The vigorous poetry even of bigotry. It was ever there in cricket, where the heroes last longer and their feats are rarely exaggerated, for there is no need. If a parish was wrecked at the fall of Oldroyd's wicket, whole states have been ruined by one over-throw – well, according to another of those nineteenth-century cricketing clergy. This time the Reverend Reynell Cotton:

Cricket

Assist, all ye Muses, and join to rehearse
An old English sport, never praised yet in verse:
'Tis Cricket I sing, of illustrious fame,
No nation e'er boasted so noble a game.
Great Pindar has bragg'd of his heroes of old –
Some were swift in the race, some in battles were
    bold:
The brows of the victor with olive were crown'd:
Hark! they shout, and Olympia returns the glad
    sound.
What boasting of Castor and Pollox his brother,
The one famed for riding, for boxing the other;
Compar'd with our heroes they'll not shine at all –
What were Castor and Pollox to Nyren and Small?
Here's to guarding and catching, and throwing and
    tossing,
And bowling and striking and running and
    crossing;
Each mate must excel in some principal part –

The Pentathlum of Greece could not show much
    art.
Ye bowlers, take heed, to my precepts attend;
On you the whole fate of the game must depend;
Spare your vigour at first, now exert all your
    strength.
But measure each step, and be sure pitch a length.
Ye fieldsmen, look sharp, lest your pains ye
    beguile;
Move close like an army, in rank and in file;
When the ball is return'd, back it sure, for I trow
Whole states have been ruin'd by one over-throw.
Ye strikers, observe when the foe shall draw nigh;
Mark the bowler, advancing with vigilant eye;
Your skill all depends upon distance and sight,
Stand firm to your scratch, let your bat be upright.
Buck, Curry and Hogsflesh, and Barbour and
    Brett,
Whose swiftness in bowling was ne'er equalled yet;
I had almost forgot, they deserve a large bumper,
Little George, the longstop, and Tom Sueter, the
    stumper.
Then why should we fear either Sackville or Mann,
Or repine at the loss both of Boynton and Lann?
With such troops as those we'll be lords of the
    game,
Spite of Minshull and Miller and Lumpy and
    Frame.
Then fill up your glass, he's the best that drinks
    most.
Here's the Hambledon Club! Who refuses the
    toast?
Let's join in the praise of the bat and the wicket,
And sing in full chorus the patrons of cricket.
And when the game's o'er and our fate shall draw
    nigh

(For the heroes of cricket, like others, must die),
Our bats we'll resign, neither troubled nor vex'd,
And give up our wickets to those who come next
Derry down, etc.

What names! Seuter the Stumper. That would be
Tom Seuter, a safe pair of Hambledon hands and a
mighty striker of a cricket ball. Barber, Hogsflesh and
Brett were bowlers, Brett the fastest and straightest
ever known, according to John Nyren. It was he who
chronicled the happenings at Hambledon, the cradle
of cricket they say, although it was only really a force
in the 1770s, 80s and early 90s. Those were days of
men like Beldham, Silver Billy Beldham. He was safer
than the Bank, said Nyren:

Silver Billy Beldham

We used to call him 'Silver Billy'. No one
within my recollection could stop a ball better, or make more brilliant hits all over the
ground. Wherever the ball was bowled, there
she was hit away, and in the most severe,
venomous style. Besides this, he was so
remarkably safe a player; he was safer than the
Bank, for no mortal ever thought of doubting
Beldham's stability. He received his instructions from a gingerbread baker at Farnham, of
the name of Harry Hall. Beldham was quite a
young man when he joined the Hambledon
Club; and even in that stage of his playing, I
hardly ever saw a man with a finer command
of his bat; but, with the instruction and advice
of old heads super-added, he rapidly attained
to the extraordinary accomplishment of being

43

the finest player that has appeared within the latitude of more than half a century. There can be no exception against his batting, or the severity of his hitting. He would get in at the balls, and hit them away in a gallant style; yet, in this single feat, I think I have known him excelled; but when he could cut them at the point of his bat, he was in his glory; and upon my life their speed was as the speed of thought. One of the most beautiful sights that can be imagined, and which would have delighted an artist, was to see him make himself up to hit a ball. It was the beau-ideal of grace, animation and concentrated energy.

The Reverend John Mitford knew Beldham well. He said that Michelangelo should have painted him. Beldham took the ball, as Burke did the House of Commons, between wind and water; not a moment too soon or late. But the men of Hambledon were not single-minded cricketers, they were often poets and singers, and one, John Small, fancied himself as a violinist. He was born in 1737 and found much favour with the Duke of Dorset, also a cricketer. Small was regarded by the duke as a fine man and a veritably entertaining musician. Indeed, the duke sent Small a violin as a present and, it is recorded, 'paid the carriage'. The last of the Hambledonians, as Pierce Egan, writing in the early nineteenth century called him:

Here lies, bowled out by death's unerring ball,
    A Cricketer renowned, by name John Small,
But though his name was Small, yet great his fame,
    For nobly did he play the noble game;

His life was like his innings, long and good,
  Full ninety summers he had death withstood.
At length the ninetieth winter came, when (fate
  Not leaving him one solitary mate)
This last of Hambledonians, Old John Small,
  Gave up his bat and ball, his leather, wax and all.

Will they write such verse about twentieth-century heroes? Certainly the skills of batsmen and the agility of fielders have calls on poetry's whimsical style. But the solid and sturdy pen of Sir Pelham – 'Plum' – Warner as he describes the youngish Don Bradman cannot but cause us to break into marching song rather than fresh-mown verse:

What were the secrets of his triumphal march through England? First, immense natural skill. Secondly, an idealism which urged him to learn everything he possibly could, and to profit by the lessons learnt. Thirdly, tremendous concentration of mind. Fourthly, physical strength. Fifthly, extreme fitness; and lastly, a cool, calm temperament. As to the actual technique of his play, he was blessed with wonderful eye, steel-like wrists, and small and beautifully neat feet, which a Genee or a Pavlova might have envied. What is his future? Is he destined to break his own records? Will he one day play an innings of 600 or 700, and put the aggregates of Grace and Hobbs, and their number of centuries, in the shade? Remember, he is only twenty-two, and, given good health, he should have at least twenty more years of cricket before him. He seems certain to plague, and at the same time delight, England's bowlers for many future seasons – indeed, boys yet unborn are destined to suffer at his hands.

Percy George Fender was not a poet. Some said he was a twentieth-century dandy. Whatever, he enjoyed life and his cricket more as some character from Cervantes than from Wisden, as Richard Streeton so perceptively remembers in his biography of one of the most attractive characters The Game has spawned:

In the closing years of his life Fender confessed he had tilted unwisely with authority for as long as he could remember, though he also believed his unconventionality was frequently only ahead of its time. The first brush with those in high places that he could recall came when he was about eleven and at St George's College, Weybridge. Fender headed the winning goal from a corner in a house match and was later reprimanded by his housemaster, whom he had expected to be pleased. 'That sort of goal is a professional's trick, Fender; no proper footballer scores a goal with his head.' Later, a century he made for St Paul's School against Bedford was not mentioned when he irritated his cricket-master by bowling lobs in the same match. A draw had looked certain and the fact that Fender snatched several wickets with his lobs and took St Paul's close to victory was considered unimportant. In county cricket the Lord's officials were not the only ground authority he upset by leading all his team through the same gate. Fender actually went further at the Oval and tried to get the Surrey amateurs and professionals to use the same dressing-room. He was dissuaded after talking with Hobbs and Strudwick. 'With respect, Mr Fender, we like to talk about you and laugh at what you might do next', was the gist of what Hobbs told him, and Fender had the perception to let the matter drop. Fender was the first man in English press boxes to use a typewriter, thus disturbing with metallic clatter traditional havens of quiet in which everyone wrote copy by hand. Fender had to ride out several storms of protest from his colleagues and once at Leeds from a persistent woman spectator sitting nearby. Fender in his most charming manner offered to type the threatened letter of complaint to the club secretary for her.

But if all that is an age gone by, then so must be Mitford's last memory of Silver Billy Beldham, who was in his nineties when John Mitford visited him in his cottage:

> Beldham still survives. He lives near Farnham; and in his kitchen, black with age, but like himself still untouched with worms, hangs the trophy of his victories; the delight of his youth, the exercise of his manhood, and the glory of his age – his BAT. Reader, believe me when I tell you I trembled when I touched it; it seemed an act of profaneness, of violation. I pressed it to my lips and returned it to its sanctuary.

We come short of the giants of old, you see. For it amuses us to trick our memories. Boys prefer heroes

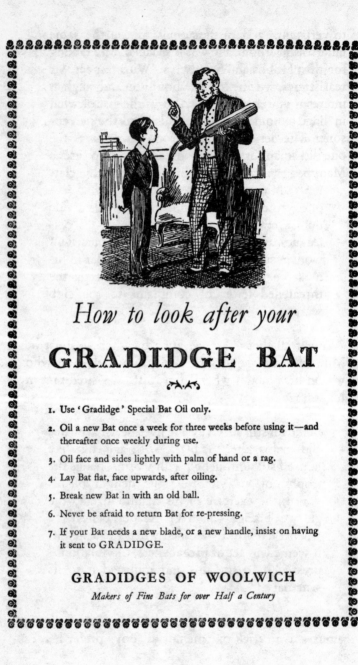

How to look after your
GRADIDGE BAT

1. Use 'Gradidge' Special Bat Oil only.
2. Oil a new Bat once a week for three weeks before using it—and thereafter once weekly during use.
3. Oil face and sides lightly with palm of hand or a rag.
4. Lay Bat flat, face upwards, after oiling.
5. Break new Bat in with an old ball.
6. Never be afraid to return Bat for re-pressing.
7. If your Bat needs a new blade, or a new handle, insist on having it sent to GRADIDGE.

GRADIDGES OF WOOLWICH
Makers of Fine Bats for over Half a Century

to verbs. They learn their cricket when heroes stand taller than any farmer's boy in the lower third. Five for thirty-one or a hundred on a turning wicket are real statistics, for no hero ever explained compound interest or logarithmic equations. No giant stood bat in hand and intoned 'nous sommes, vous êtes, ils sont.' The hero rescues us from the mundane. And one did so better than most. They called him the Old Man, and he came from Gloucester.

W. G. GRACE READY TO RECEIVE THE BALL

The Old Man and All

They say that to have played at Lord's is to have played in Heaven's cathedral of cricket. It is hallowed ground, with an inner sanctum towards which only lowered eyes may glance. When Thomas Lord established his first ground in 1781, few could have known what famous names, what mighty deeds, what reputations would be made and remembered and forgotten.

However, there were some dreadful teething troubles. As a London newspaper reported in 1814:

> A shocking accident occurred on Thursday at the new Lord's cricket ground public house, Mary-le-bone fields. The landlady of the house had occasion to use a small quantity of gunpowder, and whilst in the act of taking the

50

same from a paper, containing a pound weight, a spark from the fire caught it and it went off with a great explosion. The landlady, her sister and two little girls who were in the room were seriously burnt. The two former are in a dangerous way. The explosion broke every pane of glass in the room and also set it on fire.

And the *Morning Post* of 30 July 1825 had a further local incident to report:

DESTRUCTION OF THE ASSEMBLY, BETTING AND DRESSING ROOMS AT LORD'S CRICKET GROUNDS

About one o'clock yesterday morning a fire was discovered in the above ornamental buildings, attached to the far-famed grounds belonging formerly to Mr Lord (but now in the possession of a Mr Ward), in which, perhaps, some of the greatest cricketers have played and alternatively won and lost thousands. . . . Our reporter, who was on the spot, endeavoured by every means to find out by what accident the fire had taken place, but all he could learn was, that a party had been in the ground in the afternoon, and after their departure the rooms had been left in supposed security.

The present ground at St John's Wood was the third Lord's. Sir Spencer Ponsonby, writing in the

THE GRAPHIC

AN ILLUSTRATED WEEKLY NEWSPAPER

No. 764.—Vol. XXX.
Registered as a Newspaper

SATURDAY, JULY 19, 1884

WITH EXTRA SUPPLEMENT

PRICE SIXPENCE
By Post Sixpence Halfpenny

1. "Mistake They Make Picking Out Hulking Fellows."—2. "Don't Fret, Constance; You See, We Have the Best Eight on the River."—3. Hero-Worship: "There, Maud, That's the Highest Score Made Yet. Wouldn't You Like to Marry Him?"—4. End of Second Innings: Rush of Sweepers, Ropers, &c.—5. Running Up the Big Roller.—6. Saving Appearances: "I Say, We Must Clap Sometimes."—7. Effect of the Sun and Lunch: "Bravo, Eton; Doing Well, Eh?" "Not Very, Pa." "Dear Me! I Must Have Dreamed It.—8. Over the Garden Wall.—9. The Gentlemen's Ten Minutes.—10. Jeames's Half-Hour.

NOTES AT THE ETON AND HARROW CRICKET-MATCH

1930s, described it as it was a few years after it was set out in 1814:

> ... there was the public house, a long, low building on the south side, separated from the ground by a row of clipped lime-trees, and a few green benches on which the thirsty spectators smoked long pipes and enjoyed drinks. Round the ground there were more of these small benches without backs, and a pot-boy walked round with a supply of beer and porter for the public, who had no other means of refreshing themselves. Excepting these benches there were no seats for spectators. At the south-east corner of the ground there were large stacks of willow-blocks to be seasoned and made into bats in the workshop adjoining. On the upper north-east corner was a large sheep-pen. . . .

A sheep-pen? Such blessings for anyone who has had the drudge of preparing a rough village wicket week after week with only the bowler's moans and the batsmen's curses as thanks. Sir Spencer goes on:

> In the centre of the ground, opposite the pavilion, was a square patch of grass kept constantly rolled and taken care of. No scythe was allowed to touch it . . . the rest of the ground was ridge and furrow . . . on non-match days the public could have a pitch for a shilling which included the use of stumps, bat and ball. . . . The grass was never mowed. It was usually kept down by a flock of sheep which was penned up on match days, and on Saturdays four or five hundred sheep were

driven on to the ground on their way to the Monday Smithfield Market ... half a dozen boys picked out the rough stalks of grass. ...

Across that grass must have sped some of the hardest hit cricket balls. And oh how that wicket must have winced as the likes of Larwood thundered and hurled their ways into the history of The Greatest Game. R. C. Robertson-Glasgow saw Larwood and marvelled:

> Once, in a County match, when Larwood was in the middle of that glorious run-up, the batsman raised his hand and stopped him. Perhaps the dull reason was simply that he wasn't ready. I think, rather, that the batsman, a humble enough performer, was seized with that last love of life which must have urged victims of old to address some trivial and delaying remark to the executioner. A few seconds later the blow fell, and the bails whizzed past the wicket-keeper.

Lord's loved its heroes, especially when there was that something else, that touch that brought them close to the crowds who would smile, laugh, clap and nudge them on to another hundred, another wicket. Such a hero was Patsy Hendren. Robertson-Glasgow heard Lord's mourn his passing from The Game:

> Cricket, sometimes a rather solemn and calculating old bloke, will never forget Elias ('Patsy') Hendren. He played around cricket, and pulled at it, and called it names, and provoked it, and loved it. When he stopped playing for Middlesex cricket must have missed its imp, its laughing familiar, as Lord's

54

missed its hero. Hendren has been called a clown; but he was more like the 'Fool' who called Lear 'nuncy' and tried to keep the old man from going mad by a stream of talk that poured unmixed from the elemental humours of the earth.

But who was the greatest? Impossible to tell of course. But if it were just possible to get all the great batsmen to Lord's, say, which one would give the perfect masterclass? Imagine being able to say, 'Of course, I was coached by Bradman,' or Hutton, or Hobbs or Gunn, or Hammond or Hendren, or Ranji or Grace. Imagine, again, going up to the great man: 'Excuse me W. G., old thing, but I seem to be having this problem with my cover drive. . . .' Yet where did Grace learn his cricket? Long before he grew that shaggy beard, as he wrote himself, he:

> learned the rudiments of cricket when quite a child. As small boys we played about the gardens in a rough-and-ready way, and used to make the nurses bowl to us.

So that's where the Nursery End came from. But surely the Great Man needed no training. His was a natural talent:

> I should like to say that good batsmen are born, not made; but my long experience comes up before me, and tells me that it is not so.

he good doctor insisted on hard work and bags of sleep and a certain self-denial. Although he recognized that some might bat well after a late night, he did not recommend this regime as an alternative to clean (manly?) living:

THE CHAMPION

Ask any player who has scored over a hundred in an innings if he felt any particular influence at work on the morning of the match, and he will probably answer in the negative; but press him, and he will admit that he felt fit and well, and that the feeling was owing to a good night's rest, together with the careful training of days and weeks. I am aware that there are exceptions to this rule, and that players have been known to score largely after a night of high feasting and dancing; but in my own experience, whilst admitting that occasional freaks of this kind have been followed by moderately large scores, I cannot recollect many of my big innings that were not the results of strict obedience to the rules which govern the training for all important athletic contests. Temperance in food and drink, regular sleep and exercise, I have laid down as the golden rule, from my earliest cricketing days. I have carefully adhered to this rule, and to it in a great degree I attribute the scores that stand to my name in cricket history, and the measure of health and strength I still enjoy.

Not the most modest of statements. But then Grace believed that modesty was something to be displayed *after* a great innings, not at the time of it:

It is the first long innings that requires nerve and judgement. The hopes and fears that spring up in the young player's breast when he has scored something between fifty and a hundred make it a severe trial; and I dare say that if you and I could read his thoughts we should find that every run of the last ten was made in mental fear accompanied by a thumping heart. But when the hundred is reached, who can describe the joy that thrills him as he hears the hand-clapping and shouting!

I will not say, be modest in the hour of victory, but rather be modest after it. It is after the victory, as we listen to outside praise, that conceit and its enervating influence steal in. Turn a deaf ear, and remember it was in fear and trembling that you reached the much desired score. Quiet confidence is a widely different thing from conceit. The former will help you to a run of big scores, the latter will cripple every effort to sustain your hardly earned reputation.

W. G. Grace was a bowler as well as a batsman. As well as scoring almost 55,000 runs he took more than 2,800 wickets. And he sometimes used his forceful personality to make sure that he kept bowling. On one occasion it is said that he had been on for some considerable time when his captain, a little apprehensively, suggested a change. 'Capital idea,' said Grace, 'I'll go to the other end.' And he did.

And then there was the time, as is said in the best pavilions when the rain plays skittles with the corrugated roof, when W. G. was declared out. To the umpire, the decision was simple. The Old Man, in his somewhat high-pitched voice, had to explain: the crowd had come to see him score runs, not to see some unknown give him out.

W. G. Grace was as agile on his after-dinner feet as he was in the batting crease. R. A. Fitzgerald remembers that during the 1872 tour of Canada Grace was asked to make a series of speeches of thanks. The first was delivered in Montreal:

Gentlemen, I beg to thank you for the honour you have done me. I never saw better bowling than I have seen today, and I hope to see as good wherever I go.

The team went on to Ottawa. Up got Grace:

Gentlemen, I beg to thank you for the honour you have done me. I never saw a better ground than I have seen today, and I hope to see as good wherever I go.

And then to Toronto:

> Gentlemen, I thank you for the honour you
> have done me. I have never seen better batting
> than I saw today, and I hope to see as good
> wherever I go.

Two days later:

> Gentlemen, I have to thank you for the
> honour you have done me. I have never met
> such good fellows as I met today, and I hope I
> shall meet as good wherever I go.

The team and W. G. Grace's speech writers then
moved to Hamilton:

> Gentlemen, I have to thank you for the
> honour you have done me. I have never seen
> prettier ladies than I have seen today, and I
> hope I shall see as pretty wherever I go.

Never a man to be stuck for words, especially the
same ones, W. G. arrived in New York:

> Gentlemen, I have to thank you for the
> honour you have done me. I have never tasted
> better oysters than I have tasted here today,
> and I hope I shall get as good wherever I go.

There was rapturous applause on all occasions, or
so it is said. And what attention when the Great Man
let them into the secret of his batting:

> Do not get into the irritating habit of flour-
> ishing your bat in the air. Nothing is gained

W. G. GRACE READY TO RECEIVE THE BALL

by it, and sometimes a good deal is lost by it.

Personally, I find that the greatest scope for freedom of play is secured by holding the bat in what is called the pendulum fashion, which tends to facility of movement, without diminishing in the slightest degree the batsman's power of defence.

I await the attack of the bowler with the top of the handle of my bat just above my waist, and the bottom of the blade almost on a level with the centre of the middle stump.

Confidence comes with experience, and until confidence is acquired a batsman's defence cannot be good. An uncertain and vacillating style spells failure, for in batting he who hesitates is assuredly lost. So make up your mind how you intend playing a ball, and then play it confidently and resolutely, hitting it hard if you are going to hit, and blocking

vigorously if you intend to block. Do not
allow the bat to passively await the impact of
the ball.

So, now we all know. Yet if it was that straightforward . . . ?

But there were occasions when a sense of disappointment flitted across the image of this burly man
of Gloucester. Oscar Lloyd saw him play there. It
appears not to have been an ideal day for either of
them:

> I saw the 'Old Man' once
>> When he was old as I
> Was young. He did not score,
>> So far as I recall, a heap of runs,
> Nor even hit a four.

Oh how the mighty sometimes stumbled. It was
always so. A hundred and more years before, John
Nyren recalled the humiliation of Lumpy Stevens,
who by all accounts could bowl the greatest number
of length balls in succession. But after one game,
Lumpy Stevens met his match:

> He was a Surrey man, and lived with Lord
> Tankerville. Beyond all the men within my
> recollection, Lumpy would bowl the greatest
> number of length balls in succession. His pace
> was much faster than Lord Beauclerck's, but
> he wanted his Lordship's general knowledge
> of the game. In those days it was the custom
> for the party going from home to pitch their
> own wickets; and here it was that Lumpy,
> whose duty it was to attend to this, always

committed an error. He would invariably choose the ground where his balls would shoot, instead of selecting a rising spot to bowl against, which would have materially increased the difficulty to the hitter, seeing that so many more would be caught out by mounting of the ball. As nothing, however, delighted the old man like bowling a wicket down with a shooting ball, he would sacrifice the chances to the glory of that achievement. Many a time have I seen our General twig this prejudice in the old man when matched against us, and chuckle at it. But I believe it was almost the only mistake he ever made professional, or even moral, for he was the most simple and amiable creature. Yes – one other he committed, and many a day after the joke was remembered against him. One of our matches concluded early in the day, a long, raw-boned devil of a countryman came up, and offered to play any one of the twenty-one at single wicket for five pounds. Old Nyren told Lumpy it would be five pound easily earned, and persuaded him to accept the challenge. Lumpy, however, would not stake the whole sum himself, but offered a pound of the money, and the rest was subscribed. The confident old bowler made the countryman go in first, for he thought to settle his business in a twink; but the fellow having an arm as long as a hop-pole, reached in at Lumpy's balls, bowl what length he might; and slashed and thrashed away in the most ludicrous style, hitting his balls all over the field, and always up in the air; and he made an uncommon number of runs from this prince of bowlers before he could get him out, – and egad! he beat him! – for when Lumpy went in, not being a good batter, while the other was a very fast bowler, all along the ground, and straight to the wicket, he knocked him out presently: the whole ring roaring with laughter, and the astounded old bowler swearing he would never play another single match as long as he lived – an oath, I am sure, he religiously observed, for he was confoundedly crestfallen. Lumpy was a short man, round-shouldered, and stout. He had no trick about him, but was as plain as a pike-staff in all his dealings.

Honest, true and sturdy stock. A Hambledon man in his time was to be reckoned with. Some, like Lumpy, may have stumbled; others floated above failure. Take David Harris, a Christian soul, it is said. A devout man. A man who cast a mystic shadow as curiously as he did the small fist-clenched ball. Nyren writes:

His attitude when preparing for his run previously to delivering the ball would have made a beautiful study for the sculptor. First of all, he stood erect like a soldier at drill; then, with a graceful curve of the arm, he raised the ball to his forehead, and drawing back his right foot, started off with his left. His mode of delivering the ball was very singular. He would bring it from under the arm with a twist and nearly as high as his armpit, and with this action PUSH it, as it were, from him. How it was that the balls acquired the velocity they did by this mode of delivery I never could comprehend. In bowling he never stooped in the least in his delivery, but kept himself upright all the time. His balls were very little beholden to the ground when pitched; it was but a touch, and up again; and woe to the man who did not get in to block them, for they had such a peculiar curl, that they would grind his fingers against the bat: many a time have I seen blood drawn in this way from a batter who was not up to the trick; Old Tom Walker was the only exception – I have before classed him among the bloodless animals.

Oh the misery of failing at the wicket. The humiliation. The long walk round the boundary, to simmer, then to cool. The fists clenched in baggy pockets. The oath . . . the one unspoken, the other overheard. And the solemn plea to Him who needs no membership of the MCC. 'Lord of The Game . . . watch o'er my fate, Defend me from the swerver's puzzling flight; let me not be run out, at any rate.'

But that is the old man's prayer. It is for him who measures his devotions with all the purpose of a batsman building a big innings or a bowler knowing there is a long day in the field ahead. For the lad, there is the future and the vision of a hero who cannot fail even when there are few statistics to inscribe at the foot of the day's play. And so Oscar Lloyd's day at Gloucester was not a disappointment as he continued watching the fourless Grace:

> But still he lives before my schoolboy eye
> A giant among pygmies. In his hand
> The bag looked like a toy. I saw him stand

CAUGHT AT THE WICKET

Firm set on legs as massive as piers
Of the Norman nave at Gloucester; and the cheers
Which greeted him on the Spa were heard
As far as the Cathedral. When he stirred
The ground shook, and the crazy old
Pavilion creaked and groaned. . . .

Funny, Not Out

Why is cricket funny? Is it because it laughs at itself even when it's being pompous and foolish? And oh how delightfully pompous and foolish cricket folk can be. But they tend to keep the joke to themselves. To non-members, the humour is often as much out-of-bounds as the Long Room at Lord's. There is something in the thought that cricket was invented to infuriate foreigners. This was considered a reasonable idea when most Englishmen believed that all modern civilization rested in these islands. George Macaulay Trevelyan once noted that disinterested intellectual curiosity is the life-blood of civilization. On reflection this is perhaps why cricket spectators are generally such civilized folk. Civilized attitudes include the ability to sit alongside one another through a three-day county game and never be bored with the match or with each other's company. It must be hard to be a foreigner and not understand this. Trevelyan pitied

1. Bed of the River opposite the Twickenham Rowing Club.   2. Luncheon in the Bed of the River.   3. Cricket in the Bed of the River.

the French for not doing so: 'If the French *noblesse* had been capable of playing cricket with their peasants, their chateaux would never have been burnt.'

Geoffrey Moorhouse would have agreed.'I'm not at all surprised', he said, 'that the French have never understood this game, whose players cannot be *sérieux* when their honour is at stake. . . .' Humour and honour go together: it's a combination that avoids revolutions. (Cromwell didn't understand cricket.) To play the game is a mark of decency – of British decency, you understand. Dorothy L. Sayers explained as much when defending a member of the aristocracy accused of a most terrible crime: 'He's a damned fine cricketer and he'd no more commit murder than I would. . . .'

Americans have the hardest problem, of course. They feel they *should* understand the game and see the joke, assuming they know there's one there to see. Their problem is that they can't tolerate being left out of anything. Even more so when they don't understand what's going on. Then they become convinced that there's a conspiracy to keep them in the dark. P. G. Wodehouse, who spent so much of his time among North Americans, never lost his sense of humour. And oh how he recognised that special way in which the English could, in all innocence of course, bring so much heartache to their American cousins. Here we have Mr Crocker, an earnest American, having made the silly mistake of asking Bayliss, his host's very English butler, to explain a cricket-match report. Oh foolish man, Mr Crocker:

> It's perfectly simple, sir. Surrey won the toss and took first knock. Hayward and Hobbs were the opening pair. Hayward called Hobbs

for a short run, but the latter was unable to get across and was thrown out by mid-on. Hayes was the next man in. He went out of his ground and was stumped. Ducat and Hayward made a capital stand considering the stickiness of the wicket, until Ducat was bowled by a good length off-break and Hayward caught at second slip off a googly. Then Harrison and Sandham played out time.'

Mr Crocker breathed heavily through his nose.

'Yes!' he said, 'Yes! I had an idea that was it. But I think I'd like to have it once again, slowly. Start with these figures. What does that sixty-seven mean, opposite Hayward's name?'

'He made sixty-seven runs, sir.'

'Sixty-seven! In one game?'

'Yes, sir.'

'Why, Home-run Baker couldn't do it!'

'I am not familiar with Mr Baker, sir.'

'I suppose you've never seen a ball game?'

'Ball game, sir?'

'A baseball game?'

'Never, sir.'

'Then, Bill,' said Mr Crocker, reverting in his emotion to the bad habit of his early London days, 'you haven't lived. See here!'

Whatever vestige of respect for class distinctions Mr Crocker had managed to preserve during the opening stages of the interview now definitely disappeared. His eyes shone wildly and he snorted like a war-horse. He clutched the butler by the sleeve and drew him closer to the table, then began to move forms, spoons, cups, and even the contents of his plate, about the cloth with an energy little short of feverish.

'Bayliss?'

'Sir?'

'Watch!' said Mr Crocker, with an air of an excitable high priest about to initiate a novice into the mysteries.

He removed a roll from the basket.

'You see this roll? That's the home plate. This spoon is first base. Where I'm putting this cup is second. This piece of bacon is third. There's your diamond for you. Very well then. These lumps of sugar are the infielders and the outfielders. Now we're ready. Batter up! He stands here. Catcher behind him. Umps behind catcher.'

'Umps, I take it, sir, is what you would call the umpire?'

'Call him anything you like. It's part of the game. Now here's the box, where I've put this dab of marmalade, and here's the pitcher winding up.'

'The pitcher would be equivalent to our bowler?'

'I guess so, though why you should call him a bowler gets past me.'

'The box, then, is the bowler's wicket?'

'Have it your own way. Now pay attention. Play ball! Pitcher's winding up. Put it over, Mike, put it over! Some speed, kid! Here it comes, right in the groove. Bing! Batter slams it and streaks for first. Outfielder – this lump of sugar – boots it. Bonehead! Batter touches second. Third? No! Get back! Can't be done. Play it safe. Stick round the sack, old pal. Second batter up. Pitcher getting something

71

on the ball now beside the cover. Whiffs him. Back to the bench, Cyril! Third batter up. See him rub his hands in the dirt. Watch this kid. He's good! Lets two alone, then slams the next right on the nose. Whizzes round to second. First guy, the one we left on second comes home for one run. That's the game! Take it from me, Bill that's the game!'

Somewhat overcome with the energy with which he had flung himself into his lecture, Mr Crocker sat down and refreshed himself with cold coffee.

'Quite an interesting game,' said Bayliss, 'But I find, now that you have explained it, sir, that it is familiar to me, though I have always known it under another name. It is played a great deal in this country.'

Mr Crocker started to his feet.

'Is it? And I've been five years without finding it out! When's the next game scheduled?'

'It is known in England as rounders, sir. Children play it with a soft ball and a racket, and derive considerable enjoyment from it. I have never heard of it before as a pastime for adults.'

Two shocked eyes stared into the butler's face.

'Children?' The word came in a whisper. 'A racket?'

'Yes, sir.'

'You – you didn't say a soft ball?'

'Yes, sir.'

A sort of spasm seemed to convulse Mr Crocker. He had lived five years in England, but not till this moment had he realized to the

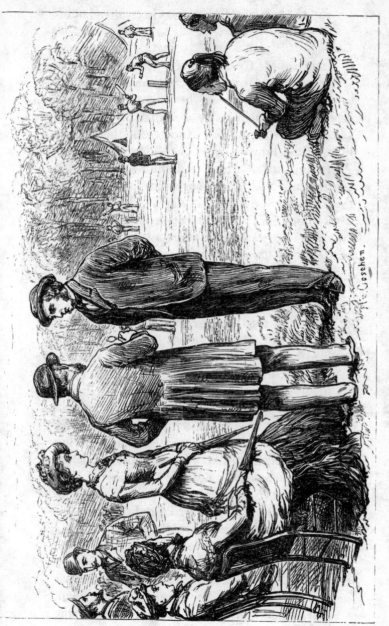

A CRICKET-MATCH AT CONSTANTINOPLE

full how utterly alone he was in an alien land.

There are Mr Crockers everywhere. It's as if those wall posters declaring that a batsman goes out to be in until he's out . . . when he comes in, are written especially for them. Why is it that explanation only adds to their confusion? Another of them, Mr Pollock, found himself in A. G. McDonnell's *England, Their England*. Mr Pollock joins a group of literary gentlemen in their charabanc south from London into the English countryside to play a village eleven. And Mr Pollock finds himself bat in hand at the wicket awaiting the ferocious doings of the enormous bowler, the village blacksmith:

> He halted at the wicket before going back for his run, glared at Mr Harcourt, who had been driven out to umpire by his colleagues – greatly to the regret of Mr Bason, the Landlord of the Shoes – glared at Mr Southcott, took another reef in his belt, shook out another inch in his braces, spat on his hand, swung his arm three or four times in a meditative sort of way, grasped the ball tightly in his colossal palm, and then turned smartly about and marched off like a Pomeranian grenadier and vanished over the brow of the hill. Mr Southcott, during these proceedings, leant elegantly upon his bat and admired the view. At last, after a long stillness, the ground shook, the grasses waved violently, small birds arose with shrill clamours, a loud puffing sound alarmed the butterflies, and the blacksmith, looking more like Venus Anadyomene than ever, came thundering over the crest. The

74

world held its breath. Among the spectators conversation was suddenly hushed. Even the urchins, understanding somehow that they were assisting at a crisis in affairs, were silent for a moment as the mighty figure swept up to the crease. It was the charge of Von Bredow's Dragoons at Gravelotte over again. But alas for human ambitions! Mr Harcourt, swaying slightly from leg to leg, had understood the menacing glare of the bowler, had marked the preparation for a titanic effort, and, for he was not a poet for nothing, knew exactly what was going on. Mr Harcourt sober had a very pleasant sense of humour, but Mr Harcourt rather drunk was a perfect demon of impishness. Sober, he occasionally resisted a temptation to try to be funny. Rather drunk, never. As the giant whirlwind of vulcanic energy rushed past him to the crease, Mr Harcourt, quivering with excitement and internal laughter, wobbling, uncertainly upon his pins, took a deep breath and bellowed 'No ball!'

It was too late for the unfortunate bowler to stop himself. The ball flew out of his hand like a bullet and hit third-slip who was not looking, full pitch on the knee-cap. With a yell of agony third-slip began hopping about like a stork until he tripped over a tussock of grass and fell on his face in a bed of nettles, from which he sprang up again with another drum-splitting yell. The blacksmith himself was flung forward by his own irresistible momentum, started out of his wits by Mr Harcourt's bellow in his ear, and thrown off his balance by his desperate effort to prevent himself from delivering the ball, and the result was that his gigantic feet got mixed up among each other and he fell heavily in the centre of the wicket, knocking up a cloud of dust and dandelion-seed and twisting his ankle. Rooks by hundreds rose in protest from the vicarage cedars. The urchins howled like intoxicated banshees. The gaffers gaped. Mr Southcott gazed modestly at the ground. Mr Harcourt gazed at the heavens. Mr Harcourt did not think the world had ever been, or could ever be again, quite such a capital place, even though he had laughed internally so much that he had got hiccups . . . .

. . . The only other incident in the innings was provided by an American journalist, by name Shakespeare Pollock, an intensively active, alert, on-the-spot young man. Mr Pollock had been roped in at the last moment to make up the eleven and Mr Hodge and Mr Harcourt had spent quite a lot of time on the way down trying to teach him the fundamental principals of the game. Donald had listened attentively and had been surprised that they made no reference to the Team Spirit. He decided in the end that the reason must have been simply that everyone knows all about it already, and that it is therefore taken for granted. Mr Pollock stepped up to the wicket in the lively manner of his native mustang, refused to take guard, on the ground that he wouldn't know what to do with it when he had got it and, striking the first ball he received towards square-leg, threw down his bat, and himself set off at a great rate in the direction of cover point. There was a paralysed silence. The rustics on the bench rubbed their eyes. On the field no one moved. Mr Pollock stopped suddenly, looked round, and broke into a genial laugh. 'Darn me – ' he began, and then he pulled himself up and went on in refined English, 'Well, well! I thought I was playing baseball.' He smiled disarmingly round.

'Baseball is a kind of rounders, isn't it, sir?' said the cover-point sympathetically.

Donald thought he had never seen an expression change so suddenly as Mr Pollock's did at this harmless, and true, statement. A look of concentrated ferocious venom obliterated the disarming smile. Cover-point, simple soul, noticed nothing, however, and Mr Pollock walked back to the wicket in silence and was out next ball. . . .

. . . The batsmen came in. The redoubtable Major Hawker, the fast bowler, thrust out his chin and prepared to bowl. In a quarter of an hour he had terrified seven batsmen, clean bowled six of them, and broken a stump. Eleven runs, six wickets, last man two. After the fall of the sixth wicket there was a slight delay. The new batsman, the local rate collector, had arrived at the crease and was ready. But nothing happened. Suddenly the large publisher, who was acting as wicket-keeper, called out.

'Hi! Where's Hawker?'

The words galvanized Mr Hodge into portentous activity. 'Quick!' he shouted. 'Hurry, run, for God's sake! Bob, George, Percy, to the Shoes!' and he set off at a sort of gallop towards the inn, followed at intervals by the rest of the side except the pretty youth in the blue jumper, who lay down; the wicket-keeper, who did not move; and Mr Shakespeare Pollock, who had shot off the mark and was well ahead of the field. But they were all late, even Mr Pollock. The gallant Major, admitted by Mr Bason through the back door, had already lowered a quart and a half of mild and bitter, and his subsequent bowling was perfectly innocuous, consisting as it did mainly of slow, gentle full pitches to leg which the village baker and even, occasionally, the rate collector hit hard and high into the long grass. The score mounted steadily.

Never mind, man, it's all part of play up and play the game. Mustn't give in. Front foot forward, elbow bent, stiff upper lip, no matter what the record of misery, ridicule and failure. There's always the next innings to show them what is what. A. P. Herbert must have pondered this as he stood a little uneasy and last man in – and not a great deal to play for:

The Ninth Wicket

The bowling looks exceptionally sound,
The wicket seems unusually worn,
The balls fly up or run along the ground;
I rather wish that I had not been born.
I have been sitting here since two o'clock;
My pads are both inelegant and hot;
I do not want what people call my 'knock',
And this pavilion is a sultry spot.
I shall not win one clap or word of praise,
I know that I shall bat like a baboon;
And I can think of many better ways
In which to spend a summer afternoon.

I might be swimming in a crystal pool;
I might be wooing some delicious dame;
I might be drinking something long and cool –
I can't imagine why I play this game.

Why is the wicket seven miles away,
And why have I to walk it all alone?
I hope Bottle's bat will drive today –
I ought to buy a weapon of my own.
I wonder if this walk will ever cease;
They should provide a motor-car or crane
To drop the batsman on the popping-crease
And, when he's out, convey him back again.
Is it a dream? Can this be truly me,
Alone and friendless in a waste of grass?
The fielding side are sniggering I see,
And long-leg sort of shudders as I pass.
I only hope no one knows my name.
I might be in a hammock with a book –
I can't imagine why I play this game.

Well, here we are, we feel a little ill.
What is this pedant of an umpire at?
Middle and off, or centre – what you will;
It cannot matter where I park the bat.
I look around me in a knowing way
To show that I am not to be cajoled;
I shall play forward gracefully and pray. . . .
I have played forward and I am not bowled.
I do not like the wicket-keeper's face.
And why are all these fielders crowding round?

The bowler makes an imbecile grimace,
And mid-off makes a silly whistling sound.
These innuendoes I could do without;
They mean to say the ball defied the bat.
They indicate that I was nearly out;

Well, darn their impudence! I know all that.
Why am I standing in this comic pose,
Hemmed in by men I should like to maim?
I might be lying in a punt with Rose –
I can't imagine why I play this game.

And there are people sitting over there
Who fondly hope that I shall make a run;
They cannot guess how blinding is the glare;
They do not know the ball is like a bun.
But, courage, heart! We have survived a ball;
I pat the pitch to show that it is bad;
We are not such a rabbit, after all:
Now we shall show them what is what, my lad!
The second ball is very, very swift;
It breaks and stands up steeply in the air;
It looks at me, and I could swear it sniffed;
I gesture at it, but it is not there.
Ah, what a ball! Mind you, I do not say
That Bradman, Hobbs, and Ranji in his prime,
Rolled into one, and that one on his day,
Might not have got a bat to it in time. . . .
But long-stop's looking for a middle-stump,
And I am walking in a world of shame;
My captain has addressed me as a chump –
I can't imagine why I play this game.

And far away, beyond the boundary, we find the
duffer. Flannels fresh, no red smear, for he is never
called upon to bowl. Shirt dry, for he survived but
one ball. But unbowed, hands unpocketed, hopes still
high because he is part of the victory and can never be
blamed for the defeat. But now, having switched off
the clock, bolted the tea-hut shutters and gathered the
flags, he is content to search for the ball, lost among
the ferns when his captain smote a mighty six. Look-

ing for the ball is an art. It is also, on occasion, a source of wonder. As E. V. Lucas noted:

In nine cases out of twelve a lost ball at cricket is found at the moment the batsman reaches the spot. The nearest fieldsman begins the hunt, then another and another join him, languidly if the game has been proceeding for some time, but zealously if it has only just begun. The bowler and batsman stand where they are and shout instructions. 'A little more to the left.' 'Try just behind you.' 'It went in line with that tree.' After a while, with a reproachful glance at the batsman, the bowler walks off. The bowler begins by looking much nearer home than the others; he does not want to flatter the batsman. At length, very slowly, but with the air of one who cannot understand how others can be so dull and blind, the batsman approaches the place, and when he is within a yard or two, the ball is found. Why this should be so is inexplicable: it is one of Nature's conjuring tricks. But if not, if the trick fails, the batsman walks on far past the others before he deigns to look on the ground at all. Was it not he who hit the ball? In very hot weather a batsman often sees the ball sink into the brake fern with a sigh of relief. Uttering a hypocritical expression of regret, he flings himself on the ground, and the longer it is before the brake fern delivers up its secret, but in no place does one hunt for a ball with more compensations, so sweet and rich and unmatchable is the scent of bruised fronds.

While brake fern is the unpleasantest, a

thicket is the worst place in which to hunt for a ball. The composition of an English thicket is five-eighths blackberry, two-eighths thorn, and one eighth stinging nettle. The question 'What is the good of stinging-nettles?', which everyone has asked at one time or another, is never so pertinent as when a ball lies, probably, in the midst of them. But the most hopeless place in which to hit is a field of standing corn. With each step you tread down so many stalks; the distance at which the ball fell is so difficult to calculate; and you have to keep one eye alert for the farmer. Standing grass is bad, but not so bad as wheat. You find strange things while looking for a lost ball: other balls lost long ago and only dimly remembered, young rabbits, fieldmice, larks' nests in the grass, and thrushes' and blackbirds' in the brambles; and a thousand and one objects so exactly like a ball from a distance that you shout the glad news. Some boys are always giving false alarms. Other boys continually ask, 'Have you got it?' 'Have you found it?' as though anyone in his senses would stay in a thicket a moment longer than is necessary. In some families a dog is trained to retrieve lost balls. In others, alack! the dog makes off with them during play. There are, of course, balls that no one can find, that never come to light again, but lie on, through the autumn, surrounded by a curious creeping life, alternately soaked by rain and blistered by the sun, until they swell and split and afford harbourage for ants or beetles, and so gradually fall to pieces and mingle with the soil.

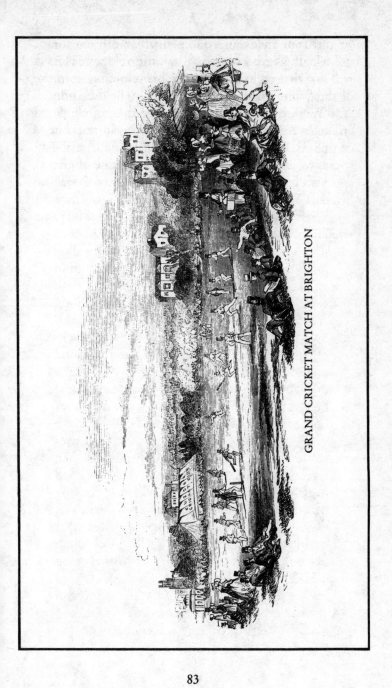

GRAND CRICKET MATCH AT BRIGHTON

83

And four fields and one hedgerow off, the rector unlocks the vestry knowing that the village cricketers will not that night be sitting in his pews, but in those of the White Hart – and more easily, he'll be bound. And English parson once remarked that mischief and cricket were queer folk and each enjoyed the other's company. But then parsons would know better than some, wouldn't they? After all, find a game of cricket and you'll find a white straw hat, slightly tilted and beneath it . . . at least a minor canon in Arlott's deckchair's gentle curve, at peace with his game which, for others passeth all understanding.

BACKING UP

The Nave that Took Spin

It was a small village, tucked into the Sussex downs. The visitors had scored 190 by tea. The village were 70 for 5 and losing heart. the wind through the late-flowering mays was damp and the grey clouds were darkening. The skipper, fearful of more wickets tumbling, brightened as rain threatened to bring his innings to an end – and a blessed draw. But the rain kept off and another wicket went down: 73 for 6. He looked across at the thin-framed, sloped and lank-haired figure. Catching his attention, he glanced up at the unobliging rain clouds.

'Hmm. Hmm. Any chance of any help then, padre!' he boomed, for he was used to giving orders. He rarely needed a favour. The parson too looked up. Blinked. Shook his head. Almost apologetically, he shook it again.

'I'm afraid not colonel,' he almost intoned. 'My influence is limited. I'm afraid we're on our own.' They were, and they lost.

The English parson sits easily in any picture of a soft summer, with chestnut tree, pretty pavilion, cool

85

lemonade jug with thin muslin cover and the warm splintery wood of the scorer's bench. Outdated yesteryear? The 1930s? No. This is from the *Church Times* of 30 June 1967:

> Old-fashioned Vicar (Tractarian) seeks colleague. Left-hand fast bowler preferred. Good golf handicap an asset but not essential. Fine church with good music tradition. Parish residential and farming. Box H. V. 521.

Now the advertiser, a Tractarian no less, knew a thing or two. A fast left-armer would have been a boon to any parish. Perhaps it was to make sure that he could baptize twins with some dexterity. Were his prayers answered? We shall never know. The country cricketing parson has a special place in The Game. Invariably he played while he was up at Oxbridge reading Greats and later Divinity. In fact he played so much that one may wonder at his intellectual powers. Firsts and Double Firsts seem to have been gained between innings. And his is always or almost always a kindly interest in The Game. Charles Dickens once found himself wandering through a soft gladed village after the two oak doors had been locked beyond Evensong:

> As I approached this spot in the evening about half an hour before sunset, I was surprised to hear the hum of voices, and occasionally a shout of merriment, from the meadow beyond the churchyard, which I found, when I reached the stile, to be occasioned by a very animated game of cricket, in which the boys and young men of the place were engaged, while the females and old people were scat-

tered about – some seated on the grass watching the progress of the game, and others sauntering about in groups of two or three, gathering little nosegays of wild roses and hedge flowers. I could not but take notice of one old man in particular, with a bright-eyed grand-daughter by his side, who was giving a sunburnt young fellow some instructions in the game, which he received with an air of profound deference, but with an occasional glance at the girl, which induced me to think that his attention was rather distracted from the old man's narration of the fruits of his experience. When it was his turn at the wicket, too, there was a glance towards the pair every now and then, which the old gentleman very complacently considered as an appeal to his judgement of a particular hit, but which a certain blush in the girl's face, and a downcast look of the bright eye, led me to believe was intended for somebody else than the old man – and understood by somebody else too, or I am much mistaken.

I was in the very height of the pleasure which the contemplation of this scene afforded me, when I saw the old clergyman making his way towards us. I trembled for an angry interruption to the sport, and was almost on the point of crying out, to warn the cricketers of his approach. He was so close upon me, however, that I could do nothing but remain still, and anticipate the reproof that was preparing. What was my agreeable surprise to see the old gentleman standing at the stile with his hands in his pockets, surveying the whole scene with evident satisfaction! And how dull must I have been not to have known till my friend the grandather (who, by-the-by, said he had been a wonderful cricketer in his time) told me that it was the clergyman himself who had established the whole thing – that it was his field they played in, and that it was he who had purchased stumps, bats, ball, and all!

A kindly soul, perhaps, who would make as if to leave his wicket when caught *before* the fielders even appealed and so to save the umpire any embarrassment should he find a decision difficult. (Except in Pakistan of course.) Beware! Not all parsons are so loved and charming. Siegfried Sassoon painted a gentle, honeysuckle-scented picture of the village flower show match. But witness the glee of the village hobbledehoy when Mr Yalden the parson loses his wicket as the church tower tolls:

The clock struck three, and the Reverend Yalden's leg-stump had just been knocked out of the ground by a vicious yorker from Frank Peckham. 'Hundred and seventeen. Five . . . Nought,' shouted the Butley scorer, popping his head out of the little flat-roofed shanty which was known as 'the pavilion.' The battered tin number plates were rattled on to their nails on the scoring board by a zealous young hobbledehoy who had undertaken the job for the day. 'Wodger say last man made?' he bawled, though the scorer was only a few feet away from him.
'Last man, Blob.'
The parson was unbuckling his pads on a bench near by, and I was close enough to

observe the unevengelical expression on his face as he looked up from under the brim of his panama hat with the MCC ribbon round it. Mr Yalden was not a popular character on the Butley ground, and the hobbledehoy had made the most of a heaven-sent opportunity.

There is, of course, nothing new in settling scores on the playing field. Imagine the bubbling excitement when the pious cassock is snared, even torn. All those years of benediction, of listening to droning sermons, of feeling guilty when, instead of contemplating the right of text and beatitude, head was bowed in thought of how to improve a drive off the back foot or even, yes even, a nurdle to leg. Norman Gale summoned so much joy when he bowled in verse not one but three cricketing curates:

The Church Cricketant

I bowled three sanctified souls
    with three consecutive balls!
What do I care if Blondin trod
    Over Niagara Falls?
What do I care for the loon in the Pit
    or the gilded Earl in the Stalls?
I bowled three curates once
    With three consecutive balls!

I caused three Protestant 'ducks'
    With three consecutive balls!
Poets may rave of lily girls
    Dancing in marble halls!
What do I care for a bevy of yachts
    Or a dozen or so of yawls?
I bowled three curates once
    With three consecutive balls!

I bowled three cricketing priests
　　With three consecutive balls!
What if a critic pounds a book
　　What if an author squalls?
What do I care if sciatica comes,
　　Elephantiasis calls?
I bowled three curates once
　　With three consecutive balls!

Let's not be too harsh on sanctified souls. After all they too have averages in this life as well as the next. And many have had an eye for a good wicket wherever they may have been. Richard Lloyd, the organist at Durham Cathedral, remembered that an earlier dean of that place did not always allow his thoughts to be dragged from the mown and rolled wickets. The then Dean, Dr Cyril Alington, often wondered on matters more earthly than heavenly. He once admitted that, in procession, his first thought was, would the nave take the spin? It is to the precincts of the parson's workplace that Edmund Blunden trod and glanced and stooped and read for further memory. The graveyard holds so many secrets, its tenants forever silent on the great deeds they claimed were theirs. Was it really a catch? Did he really get a touch? Blunden found the headstone of a man of the cloth much loved in the parish, although not always held in such affection when other men came to the village only to be stumped by the Reverend wicket-keeper or thrashed to the furthest boundary when it was his turn to bat:

Biographical information on any man's gravestone has been growing sparser lately than I could wish. I have a passion for it. I love to be allowed a little more to see of the men and women who once enjoyed life, or experienced it at least, than bare names and chronology allow. It may be nothing to them; as Thomas Hardy felt when he wrote the wonderful elegiac song, 'Friends Beyond', but it is something to us who can still consider 'the moral and the mystery of the man'. Somewhere I read the last letter of a man who was about to be hanged for murder, and as I remember it, it bore the postscript, 'No more cricket, George.' If that were added to any inscription which indicated the other part of the story, it might be a voice from the tomb which would not require the old preamble 'Stop, passer-by.' Our cordial parson, to come back to the upper side of the daisies, was well known in many a cricket field besides our own, and in higher company than local matches attracted; sometimes, it may be, he put over an old sermon because the week's demands on him and his cricket bag had given no time for writing the new one. ('How did you like the sermon?' 'I like it better every time I hear it.') I only know of one cricketer who could combine the most able attention to a terrific match with the writing of something as remote from it as the works of Sir Thomas Browne. It was not our old friend. He put on his white sun-hat with a single purpose, a first great Cause. The vicar was a wicket-keeper of heavy build but a light and menacing rapidity in action. As had been hinted, he did not spare the foolish and they say he played some tricks on his slower-thinking adversaries. I saw him once stump a batsman with such utter speed and indolence mixed as Ames of Kent in later days could show when Freeman lured the striker out of his ground – but the vicar's chance on the occasion I noted was the briefest imaginable. When his turn came to swing the bat he attacked the ball with a vengeance other than the Lord's, but possibly a theologian could explicate a relationship and justify the vicar's own Article. A slovenly bad ball, 'a godly and wholesome doctrine' of driving it and all such out of the earth. As he grew old, and fell lame, the world underwent changes which he did not find easy – who did? There was local change which must often have grieved him when he looked forth from the fine vicarage windows southward into that lustrous light which is so often found over the valley there. The cricket ground, scene of so many of his deeds and quips and social inter-changes, had been ploughed up during the First World War, and was no longer used except by fat sheep cleaning up kale. The velvety greensward, the music of the bat well used, the laugh at the unfortunate 'leather-hunter' on a hot chase, the bearded mower going to and from behind the horse in his leather shoes, the old men commending or disrelishing play from the bench by the oak, the call from the pavilion that sent the tins hustling up on the scoreboard, the players arriving with their radiant caps and blazers, or strolling out to the pitch with bare heads catching the sunlight, the deck chairs, the teacups, the gentle ladies who presided over them – none there any more. Just stripped, untidy stems of kale.

A man of some determination and learning, and perhaps a mourner for those things that mattered and had gone by. Sad, but we must thank the chronicles of many a parson with time and inclination to record the earliest days of the game. And what days they were! The Reverend Pycroft, writing in the mid-nineteenth century, presents an astonishing scene of whizzing cricket balls and flashing blades – and all without need of vinegar and brown paper:

> At Oxford I once could see, any day in summer, on Cowley Marsh, two rows of six wickets each facing some other, with a space of about sixty yards between each row, and ten yards between each wicket. Then, you have twelve bowlers and as many hitters – making twelve balls and twenty-four men, all in danger's way at once, besides bystanders. the most any one of these bowlers can do is to look out for the ball of his own set; whether hit or not by a ball from behind, is very much a matter of chance. A ball from the opposite row once touched my hair! The wonder is, that twelve balls should be flying in a small space nearly every day, yet no man hit in the face.

All this and not a helmet or an arm-guard to be seen. Nor was there thirty or so years earlier when Mary Russell Mitford, was writing about her village, where they'd played cricket since the eighteenth century. Of course the parson was there to play the match, if not to see it fairly played. It was a time of fun that brought forth apple-dunking mirth on the cricket field that was never smooth, never the same, never hallowed, and, on this occasion, very wet:

R. KYNASTON, ESQ.

William Grey made a hit which actually lost the cricket-ball. We think she lodged in a hedge, a quarter of a mile off, but nobody could find her. And George Simmons had

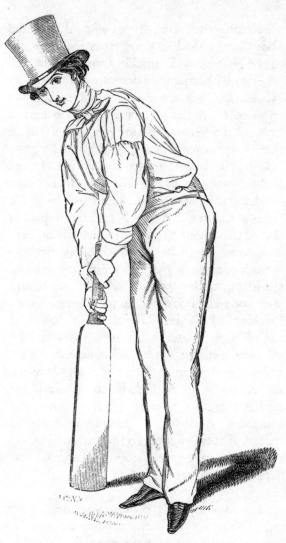

C. TAYLOR, ESQ.

nearly lost his shoe, which he had tossed away
in passion, for having been caught out, owing
to the ball glancing against it. These, together
with a very complete somersault of Ben

Appleton, our long-stop, who floundered about in the mud, making faces and attitudes as laughable as Grimaldi (none could tell whether by accident or design), were the chief incidents of the scene of action. Among the spectators nothing remarkable occurred beyond the general calamity of two or three drenchings, except that a form placed by the side of the hedge, under a very insufficient shelter, was knocked into the ditch, in a sudden rush of the cricketers to escape a pelting shower, by which means all parties shared the fate of Ben Appleton, some on land and some by water: and that, amidst the scramble, a saucy gipsy of a girl contrived to steal from under the knee of the demure and well apparelled Samuel Long, a smart hand-kerchief which his careful dame had tied round it to preserve his new (what is the mincing feminine word?) – his new inexpres-sibles, thus reversing the story of Desdemona, and causing the new Othello to call aloud for his handkerchief, to the great diversion of the company. And so we parted; the players retired to their supper, and we to our homes; all wet through, all good-humoured and happy – except the losers.

We must suppose the parson was there, perhaps casting a benign eye, hands clasped behind frock-coated back, and not pointed in solemn accusation. For all his dignity of office and the worthiness of his calling, the parson rarely stands in judgement on his fellow cricketers. That is for one in buttoned not flowing surplice, for one armed with tablets not from God but from the earthly umpire, Lord's.

AN ANXIOUS MOMENT

On Hallowed Ground

It might have been 1907, maybe the year before. Anyway it was at Lord's. Kent were playing Middlesex and Lord Harris was having something to say about the umpiring. Lord Harris usually had something to say about the umpiring. He turned the conversation to a man called Henry Royston, a bowler in his time before he took up umpiring. Well, according to Lord Harris (in those days things were often according to Lord Harris) Royston gave a very famous batsman out, run out, even though it was clear to everyone there that the Great Man had been well in his crease.

'Why was he out?' asked his lordship.

He was encouraged to continue. The umpire, it seems, had felt that there wasn't much time left for the

game and if the batsman had survived for much
longer, then the fielding side had no chance of winning. Royston did not think much of this situation,
hence the somewhat dubious decision.

'We're obliged', said Royston, 'to study them
things you know, else 'ow are we a going to win our
matches?'

How else indeed? The umpire is the grim reaper of
cricket. Once upon a time he would even wear a black
– not a white – coat. He stands in terrible judgement

A CLEAR CASE

on the mighty as well as the sloggers and cross-batters. No one is beyond his raised finger. On the pitch he is God: how appropriate that the umpire's finger never points accusingly, but heavenwards. But oh how he is sometimes loathed for no other reason than a batsman's ineptitude or a bowler's bad chance. A. G. Steel wrote in late Victorian times that it was a thankless task to stand where others would not:

> If anyone were to ask us the question, 'What class of useful men receive most abuse and least thanks for their service?' we should, without hesitation, reply, 'Cricket umpires'. The duties of an umpire are most laborious and irksome; they require for their proper performance the exercise of numerous quali-fications, and yet it is always the lot of every man who dons the white coat, the present dress of an umpire, to receive, certainly no thanks, and, too frequently, something which is not altogether unlike abuse.

Where did this sad figure come from? Surely no man would volunteer for such abuse? Originally he was the notcher, a crouching figure at the edge of the field. He sat close by and simply notched the score on a piece of wood as a non-stipendary arbiter of the play. In the late 1770s it was decided that umpires were not only necessary, they needed a set of Laws – not rules, but Laws – to give them authority:

Laws for Ye Umpires

Umpires are sole judge of all Outs and Ins, of all fair and unfair play, of frivolous delays, of all hurts, whether real or pretended, and are discretionally to allow what time they think proper before ye game goes on again.

In case of real hurt to a Striker, they are to allow another to come in and ye Person hurt to come in again, but are not to allow a fresh Man to play, on either side, on any Account.

They are the sole judge of all hindrances, crossing ye Players in running, standing unfair to strike, and in case of hindrance may order a Notch to be scored.

They are not to order any Man out unless appealed to by one of ye players.

These laws are to ye Umpires jointly.

Each Umpire is ye sole judge of all Nips and Catches, Ins and Outs, good or bad Runs, at his own Wicket, and his determination shall be absolute, and he shall not be changed for another Umpire without ye consent of both Sides.

When ye 4 Balls are bowled, he is to call Over.

When both Umpires shall call Play, 3 times, 'tis at ye peril of giving ye Game from them that refuse to play.

In Hampshire in the 1860s A. G. Steel came across a very jolly man who by his very good nature sometimes felt the need to ignore the letter of the Laws for reasons that were nothing to do with the game of Hambledon:

The village umpire there, a jolly, good-natured old man, but absolutely ignorant of the laws of cricket, caused us the greatest merriment during the whole day. In addition

100

to his official post as umpire, he was the village caterer at all public entertainments, and consequently supplied the luncheon at all the matches. It was evident his thoughts in the field were divided between the responsibilities of his two duties – at least we inferred so by his occasionally allowing the bowler to bowl as much as ten or more balls an over, and giving as his reasons, 'If Mr A. doant have a bot o' exercise, he won't relish my steak pie. O'im vaamous for steak pies, yer know sir,' he added by way of apology for introducing the subject.

It is a rotten lot to stand, over after over, in weather foul and shivering and then, when the gentle sun warms the field, to become a hook for sweaters and caps. And then, buried beneath a veritable changing room of woolly smells, to be expected to watch foot and line and bounce and swerve and pitch and nick and . . . to give sober, calm judgement. And when wrong or wrongfully abused, to stand passively by, to show no temper nor side nor distress. Should there be lunch and tea, then the two white-coated figures must eat alone away from the joshing and gossip until it is time to go out once more, instead of passing the time of evening's play with friends. And if there is a batsman's disappointment to face at the close of play, or the fury of a bowler in full flight and screaming appeal, then so be it.

So fierce was the bowling of Jack Crossland, and so aggressive his appeals, that nineteenth-century umpires of the day were afraid to question his action, even the fact that he bowled unfairly on occasions: he threw. By 1883, our Lord Harris, even then with something to say about umpires, announced that as the wretched fellows were reluctant to penalize bowlers then he, Harris, would propose new wording to the laws of cricket to force an umpire to yell, or more modestly, call, 'No Ball'. Let no one think that doubtful umpires stood only on England's pleasant fields. W. G. Grace, recalling his tours of Australia towards the end of the 1800s, had a few things to say that would have had Lord Harris nodding in agreement:

> Australia has always been deficient in the matter of good umpires, and though we in England are by no means perfect in this respect, the Australians are a long way behind us. In those days professional umpires were almost unheard of in Australia. Anyone who took an intelligent interest in cricket was thought good enough to umpire. Consequently inexperienced men had the delicate and onerous duty thrust upon them, with the result that no confidence was placed in their judgement and scant respect was paid to their decisions. I attribute the friction which has frequently arisen during the visits of the English teams to Australia to the fact that even at the present time Australia is not well provided with good umpires. When I first played in Australia there were not sufficient important matches to keep capable umpires employed. The matches between Victoria and New South Wales were the only really important events in the cricket calendar – there was no South Australian team then. Even now, except when an English Team visits Australia, first-class matches are few and far between, though, of course, there is plenty of club

cricket. In England we draw our umpires from the ranks of professional cricketers of long experience, who have retired from active participation in the game; but in Australia they have not professional cricketers in sufficient number to keep up the supply of efficient umpires. It is not always recognized that the duties of an umpire call for uncommon intelligence, decisive judgement, and intimate acquaintance with the laws and customs of the game. It is too often assumed that because a man has been a good cricketer he is sure to make a good umpire, but I contend that this is no criterion, and that a more necessary qualification for an umpire is that he should have a good head on his shoulders, and should have had constant practice at this special branch of work.

Whatever W. G. Grace thought of Australian umpires, migration to the northern hemisphere was no certain protection. A. G. Steel spoke of a game towards the end of the last century, where the local laird fancied himself as something of a batsman. Like so many Scottish things cricket was a family affair, and that included his lordship's manservant. Now, the goodly retainer could not expect to play. After all, he might have out-batted, out-bowled or even out-fielded his master. So, what to do? Why, umpire of course. In that way the estate was in safe hands. Steel was bemused by one incident. The landed batsman was playing and missing, as the delightful jargon has it. He had survived an enormous number of very reasonable appeals for LBW and catches at the wicket. On the last ball of the over, his lordship bent his knee almost to the ground as if to prepare himself for some well-deserved dubbing by the monarch. The ball struck with a thud: 'Not out . . . '

> . . . the writer ventured humbly to ask the umpire whether the last appeal (an enormous thigh right in front of all three stumps, to a straight one) had not been a very near thing.
> 'Lor bless you sir,' was the reply, 'I have been his valet for fifteen years, and I dussn't give him out; he gets awful wild at times.'

Perhaps it is because umpires have all reached a certain age before buttoning on that white flapping coat (they rarely quite manage to look like house surgeons, do they?) that they have so much character. In the villages they are invariably sharp of wit and, sometimes, the butt of the young, who sadly never saw their grand deeds, accomplished before the tell-tale limp of a pounded knee meant that gussetted flannels were needed no more. The young Siegfried Sassoon preserved two such characters in his *Memoirs of a Fox-Hunting Man*. Messrs Seamark and Sutler came from fiction – or did they? They might just have been real people, standing as village umpires not far from Paddock Wood in Kent during the 1890s and very early 1900s.

> The umpires in their long white coats have placed the bails on the stumps, each at his own end, and they are still satisfying themselves that the stumps are in the requisite state of exact uprightness. Tom Seamark, the Rother-den umpire, is a red-faced sporting publican who bulks as large as a lighthouse. As an umpire he has certain emphatic mannerisms. When appealed to he expressed a negative

decision with a severe and stentorian 'NOT OUT': but when adjudicating that the batsman is out, he silently shoots his right arm towards the sky – an impressive and irrevocable gesture which effectively quells all adverse criticisms. He is, of course, a tremendous judge of the game, and when not absorbed by his grave responsibilities he is one of the most jovial men you could meet with.

Bill Sutler, our umpire, is totally different. To begin with, he has a wooden leg. Nobody knows how he lost it; he does nothing to deny the local tradition that he was once a soldier, but even in his cups he has never been heard to claim that he gave his limb for Queen and Country. It is, however, certain that he is now a cobbler (with a heavily waxed moustache) and a grossly partisan umpire. In direct contrast to Tom Seamark he invariably signifies 'Not out' by a sour shake of the head; when the answer is an affirmative one he bawls 'Hout' as if he'd been stung by a wasp. It is reputed that (after giving the enemy's last man out leg-before in a closely-fought finish) he was once heard to add in an exultant undertone: 'And I've won my five bob.' He has also been accused of making holes in the pitch with his wooden leg in order to facilitate the efforts of the Butley bowlers.

But who gives the umpire out? Who has the courage and judgement of that abused figure? Who has the steady hand that can gently pat a village's thanks on an old man's white-coated shoulder and know the right words that say the time has come to stand no longer in the middle meadow? Bertram Atkey knew an old man of the West Country. He'd heard the rumours. But Mr Joseph Nicholas, Umpire, refused to walk.

Mr Joseph Nicholas – Umpire

Thee can'st ask me t'bowell 'r ask me t'bat, thee
     can'st
   ask me t' vield if thee'st like.
But I'll answer thee sharp that I wants none o'
   that, fer at they things I goes out on strike!
Haw! Haw! I goes out on strike!
   Fer I bain't such a vool as t' make meself sweat
      wi'
a-bowellin' th' ball 'r a-hettin' 'un.
   I'll stan' at th' wickets 'n' watch a ball het – but
I sartinly sha'n't start a gettin' 'un!
   'Pend 'pon 't I sha'n't start a-gettin' 'un.

I've umpired out team fer nigh thirty year, 'n'
   I've won 'em their games be the dozen,
'N' they'd sooner I umpired that ar'n aroun' 'ere –
   fer they knows as they'd soon git a wuzz'n!
Be Jarge! they'd soon git a wuzz'n!
   W'y; 'twur I gi'ed 'em Ben Bundy out 'leg-afore'
vive year ago come next Michael'as
   W'en Charlton-cum-Britford 'ad two more
      t'score – 'n'
th' team they gi'ed three cheer fer Nicholas.
   Be Jarge! 'Ow they cheered fer 'Joe Nicholas'!
'Oo wur it said as 'twur' time t'stop play w'en
   Landford last year nerly won?
W'wy, I wur th' man, 'n' I drawed stumps that day
      –
   'n' Lor! 'ow I 'ad t' run!

106

They Lanford chaps made me run!
　　But I clung t' th' stumps 'n' I runned like a
hare – 'twur a turrible chase I led –
　　　'N' we won thic' match wi' an hour t' spare – fer
　　　　I
hid 'em under me bed!
　　Th' stumps they went under me bed!

I was telled as 'ow one o' them young fellers swore
　　as I didn't know th' rools o' th' game!
W'y, I've 'ad 'em in print iver since '74 – so I
　　very soon put he t' shame!
'Old rot 'un! I put he t' shame!
　　All 'is new-fangled notions about 'leg-afore' I
didn't hold wi' 'em at all!
　　　'N' I argued th' p'int fer an hour 'r more – 'n' I
　　　　made
'un look turrible small!
　　'Old rot un! I made un look small

'E said 'if th' ball breaks 'n' hets th' man's laig
　　it's th' umpire's juty t' call
"Not Hout!" 'N' I answers sarcusstic, 'I baig t'
　　state Hi sh'd holler "New Ball!"
'N' dammee! I'd 'ave a new ball!
　　Fer 'ow ye cud play wi' a ball that was broke is
licker, my lad, t' me!'
　　　'N' th' feller 'e passed it all off as a joke –
but that's 'ow I finished he!
　　Ay! That's 'ow I polished off he!

Still, I've 'eard as there's talk o' 'resignin' me
　　fer a younger 'n' cunnin'er man,
But there'll on'l be one umpire 'ere – you'll see –
　　fer as long as I'm able t' stan'
I'll be umpire w'ile I kin stan'!
　　'N' th' very nex' match as the village do play

will commence wi' me in me pleace,
     'N' then if th' fellers got aught t' say – kin
say it straight t' me feace!
     Do 'ee see? Say – it – straight – t' – me feace!

A Boys' Own Game

Watching from the wood-backed seats in the members' stand, he looked almost a frail figure. The innings was over and the other fielders were hurrying to the pavilion. Some stopped to sign scorecards for the small boys who swarmed like urgent beggars during the few seconds that the home side neared the players' gate. He was hanging back. It was his first game for the county side. He was in no hurry to leave the field. He looked a little embarrassed. He watched two of the senior men – one had played for England – as they firmly walked by the outstretched autograph books. He made for the gate. Then one tee-shirted urchin figure, disappointed perhaps, turned and saw him for the first time. He kept on walking, hurrying now, eyes lowered. A voice at his elbow said, 'Give us yer name mister.' Hardly stopping, he fumbled at the gaudy blue book and the sticky felt-tip and scribbled quickly, forgetting the hours of practice, the careful shaping of the sweeping 's' and the line and two dots beneath. The boy said thanks. He didn't really hear him. Tripping almost, he was inside the gate and into the dressing room. He was red-faced and didn't dare look at the other players. He'd signed his first autograph.

As W.G. remarked, there's only a need for modesty after the event. Some players, used to more sheltered backgrounds, have never wanted to be heroes off the field. Take the South African player N. A. Quinn. He'd had a good tour in Australia. He'd taken a lot of wickets and he'd taken more than his fair share of barracking as a result. Truthfully, Quinn was getting fed up with the public side of being a tourist. He'd sooner have been home in South Africa. The worst of it was the continuing demands of the autograph hunters who flocked about the players like penny insurance salesmen. Bowling at Bradman, and very successfully too, was one thing; facing autograph hunters was another. He'd been told that this however was part of the deal of being famous. One evening he'd just come out of the Melbourne cricket ground when yet another figure, this time a scrawny, bare-legged young girl, thrust book and pencil beneath his nose. 'Sign this will yer mate?' she said with an authority learned at her brother's elbow. Dressed in grey suit and wide-brimmed hat to conceal his identity, Quinn almost panicked. He cleared his throat. 'Hmm, Hmm. I'm not a cricketer young lady,' he tried. Her blue eyes never blinked. 'I know that Mr Quinn,' she said, 'But I'd like yer moniker all the same.'

Two levels of hero worship. For it is the youngster who really knows The Game. The gentleman, and now the players, may sit in the Long Room and mutter about whether it was J. F. G. W. Baggerston-Rees who failed to get his Blue in 1933. The school-boys have no need for such initials or debates. They

110

OUR NATIONAL GAME

are the real experts. They know the worth of those in the Long Room, both the quick and the dead. But let us not suppose that all schoolboys cherish Wisden before *Beano*. Arthur Marshall, in his memoirs, has a different memory of enforced cricket at school:

> Cricket did have one supreme advantage over football. It could be stopped by rain. Every morning at prayers, devout cricket-haters put up a plea for a downpour. As we were in England, our prayers were quite frequently answered, but nothing, nothing but the death of the headmaster, could stop football. We could hardly pray for the headmaster, a nice man, to die. In rain, sleet, hail and lightning, shivering and shuddering and soaked to the skin, we battled on. Even in dense fog we kept at it, a shining example to Dartmoor working parties. But cricket was another matter, cricket was a more sensitive affair altogether, and if, as I fear, there is cricket in heaven, there will also, please God, be rain.

Hardly *Boys' Own* stuff from Mr Marshall. Yet the agony of the very unsporting schoolboy, the non-cricketer, is only matched by the slumped hopes of the lad whose bat was not quite straight enough to block the yorker. To the twelve-year-old, all yorkers are full tosses waiting to be hit. And what of the gangling youth who neither bats nor bowls? All afternoon, with one eye on his skipper, he fields wherever he's told. He is the confirmed duffer, as W. G. Grace called him:

> What to do with a 'duffer' is a knotty problem which I cannot pretend to have solved. In the old days, when I was a young cricketer, we

always used to put him at short-leg, but why I never could conceive, because if there is one place where you may get a harder catch than another, it is at short-leg. On the whole, I think the easiest position in the field, and the one to which I should give the duffer his place, is mid-on, for though the ball may come quickly to that fieldsman, it generally comes straight from the bat. But, of course, everything depends upon who is bowling and batting. While one batsman is at the wicket a particular fielder may find his place a perfect sinecure, whereas with the very next man in he may be kept perpetually leather-hunting.

Surely the duffer at whatever age is to be encouraged, isn't he? A kindly word from his housemaster, a helping tip from his captain, an extra hour in the nets with his elder brother. For some, though, there is nothing but hope in spite of the knowledge of his peers that although it springs eternally on the cricket field it too often spells gloom. R. C. Robertson-Glasgow played fine cricket at Oxford and then for Somerset. When he took up his pen he recalled one young fellow who was not – quite – a duffer:

The One Way Boy

When coaching boys the other day,
Recalling legs that legward stray,
Wearily pleading that it mars
The style, if bats are scimitars;
Persuading bowlers that their length
And rectitude are more than strength,
However jovially applied
If all it ends in is – a wide,
The father of some cricketer,

A heavy man, approach'd, said, 'Sir,
My boy is always caught at slip;
It gives me one gigantic pip:
Now can you give me any reason
Why this should happen all the season,
Instead of intermittently,
As it occurs with you or me?'
'Show me the boy,' quoth I, 'sir please.'
Whereat, scorbutic, ill-at-ease,
Stole from behind his ample father
A boy obscured till now, or rather
What might have passed for boy, by chance,
But for his cow-like countenance:
Never in any town or rank
Saw I a face so wholly blank:
No freckle, twinkle; nothing dimply;
It was facial Sahara, simply.
'Put on those pads,' his father said
As if conversing with the dead,
'And show the gentleman the stroke,
Concerning which I lately spoke.'
He donned them filially resign'd.
I gave him guard, to leg inclined,
I bowled him long hops free from guile,
Full-pitchers you could hit a mile,
Half-volleys straight, half-volleys wide,
Swervers, delicious for the glide;
He never swerved, or lost his grip,
But snicked the ruddy lot to slip.
Strange wonders have there been in Cricket –
Once, in a match, I took a wicket,
Shod in a heel-less evening shoe
(A confidence 'twixt me and you),
Jones bowled a ball through Grace's beard,
And Ranji only Lockwood feared,
But never, since the game began,

Since old men stood while young men ran,
Was such consummate batsmanship
As to hole out, each ball, at slip.
'Take off those pads,' his father said
(Resuming converse with the dead),
'You've shown the gentleman the stroke
By which my heart and mother's broke;
Good-day Sir!' and with footsteps slow
He took his tragedy in tow,
The parent first, the portent after,
Leaving me deep in awe and laughter.

GOING IN

Never mind. As that old Sussex village cricketer Pondweed Philcox used to say in his sober moments, 'You've got to know when to nurdle 'em.' The problem, of course, is that a lad who plays up and plays this greatest of all games is no longer a boy once he treads from the pavilion's rickety steps. The ball is hard, the bat firm, the gentlest return catch bruising. A game for men even when played by boys. At his school, Arthur Marshall shuddered at the very thought of this maturity at such a tender age and disposition:

It always seemed to me, as a schoolboy reluctantly playing cricket in the 1920s, that a straight bat, so highly prized by the experts, was in my case mere foolishness, sending the ball, when I managed to make contact with it, feebly back whence it had come. With a crooked bat there was at least a chance of deflecting the offensive weapon either to the right or left and scoring a 'run'. To attempt to score anything at all may savour of self-advertisement but that was never my aim. My sights were not set on a ribboned coat or a captain's hand on my shoulder smote. The sole purpose of a run was to remove me, however briefly, from the end where the action was. Cricket was a manly game. Manly masters spoke of 'the discipline of the hard ball'. Schools preferred manly games. Games were only manly if it was possible while playing them to be killed or drowned or, at the very least, badly maimed. Cricket could be splendidly dangerous. Tennis was not manly, and if a boy had asked permission to spend the afternoon playing croquet he would have been instantly punished for his 'general attitude'. Athletics were admitted into the charmed lethal circle as a boy could, with a little ingenuity, get impaled during the pole-vault or be decapitated by a discus and die a manly death. Fives were thought to be rather tame until one boy ran his head into a stone buttress and got concussion and another fainted dead away from heat and fatigue. Then everybody cheered up about fives. The things to aim at in games were fright and total exhaustion. It was felt that these, coupled with a diet that was only modestly calorie-laden, would keep our thoughts along the brightest and most wholesome lines. As a plan, this was a failure. For cricket matches against other schools, the school pavilion was much in evidence. At my preparatory school, Stirling Court on the Hampshire coast, the pavilion smelt strongly of linseed oil and disinfectant and for its construction reliance had been largely placed upon corrugated iron. Within could be found cricket nets and spiders and dirty pads and spiders and old team photographs and spiders. There was also a bat signed by Hobbs which we proudly displayed to opposing players in an unconscious spirit of gamesmanship. But despite this trophy, a sad air of failure and decay pervaded the building. From its windows innumerable cricketing disasters had been witnessed: for example, our defeat by Dumbleton Park when our total score had been eight, three of which were byes. There had been, too, the shaming afternoon when our captain, out first ball, had burst into a torrent of hysterical tears.

Others, though, dreamed of their colours, the first cast of the linseed oil cloth over yellowed bat, the school clock chimes that would release them from penitential irregular verbs to the freedom of a closely barbered square and news of the county's lunchtime score. Long ago, did not Thomas Moult gaze above the droned conjugations to the loveliest of our English games?:

There's music in the names I used to know,
And magic when I heard them, long ago.

'Is Tyldesley batting?' Ah, the wonder still!
 . . . The school clock crawled, but cricket-thoughts
    would fill
The last slow lesson-hour deliciously.
(Drone on, O teacher: you can't trouble me.)
'Kent will be out by now' . . . (well, if you choose
To keep us here while cricket's in the air,
You must expect our minds to wander loose
Along the roads to Leicester, Lord's and Leeds,
Old Trafford and the Oval, and the Taunton
    meads. . . .)

And then, at last, we'd raid the laneway where
A man might pass, perchance, with latest news.
Grey-grown and grave, yet he would smile to hear
Our thirsty questions as we crowded near.
Greedily from the quenching page we'd drink –
How its white sun-glare made our young eyes
    wink!
'Yes, Tyldesley's batting still. He's ninety-four.
Barlow and Mold play well. Notts win once more.
Glo'ster (with Grace) have lost to Somerset –
East: ten wickets: Woods and Palairet. . . .'
So worked the magic in that summer lane.
The stranger beamed. Maybe he felt again
As I feel now to tell the linked names
Jewelling the loveliest of our English games.
Abel and Albert Trott, Lilley, Lillywhite,
Hirst, Hearne, and Tunnicliffe – they catch the
    light –
Lord Hawke and Horny, Jessop, A. O. Jones –
Surely the glow they held was the high sun's!

Or did a young boy's worship think so
And is it but his heart that's aching now?

CRICKET-MATCH AT WINCHESTER BETWEEN ETON AND WINCHESTER COLLEGES

119

Far from the municipal rec. and the milk-crate stumps. Yet the game is just as important. The one-padded scamp can still be Botham, Hutton, Compton, Bradman, Hammond or Hobbs. The bouncing compo ball may yet fly from the unsteady hand of a budding Holding, Snow, Truman, Larwood, Freeman or Grimmett. But only in the imagination does the school first eleven take on the men from London. Or in fiction. Remember how Tom Brown's side at Rugby played the gentlemen from the MCC:

'Oh well bowled! Well bowled, Johnson!' cries the captain, catching up the ball, and sending it high above the rook trees, while the third Marylebone man walks away from the wicket, and the old Bailey gravely sets up the middle stump again and puts the bails on.

'How many runs?' Away scamper three boys to the scoring-table, and are back again in a minute amongst the rest of the eleven, who are collected together in a knot between wicket. 'Only eighteen runs, and three wickets down!' 'Huzza, for old Rugby!' sings out Jack Raggles, the long-stop, toughest and burliest of boys, commonly called 'Swiper Jack'; and forthwith stands on his head, and brandishes his legs in the air in triumph, till the next boy catches hold of his heels and throws him over on to his back. 'Steady there, don't be such an ass, Jack,' says the captain, 'we haven't got the best wicket yet. Ah, look out now at cover-point,' adds he, as he sees a long-armed, bare-headed, slashing-looking player coming to the wicket. 'And, Jack, mind your hits; he steals more runs than any man in

England.' And they all find that they have got their work to do now; the newcomer's off-hitting is tremendous and his running like a flash of lightning. He is never in his ground, except when his wicket is down. Nothing in the whole game is so trying to boys; he has stolen three byes in the first ten minutes, and Jack Raggles is furious, and begins throwing over savagely to the farther wicket, until he is sternly stopped by the captain. It is all that young gentleman can do to keep his team steady, but he knows that everything depends on it, and faces his work bravely. The score creeps up to fifty, the boys begin to look black, and the spectators, who are now mustering strong, are very silent. The ball flies off his bat to all parts of the field, and he gives no rest and no catches to anyone. But cricket is full of glorious chances and the goddess who presides over it loves to bring down the most skilful players. Johnson, the young bowler, is getting wild, and bowls a ball almost wide to the off; the batter steps out and cuts beautifully to where cover-point is standing very deep, in fact, almost off the ground. The ball comes skimming and twisting along about three feet from the ground; he rushes at it, and it sticks somehow or other in the fingers of his left hand, to the utter astonishment of himself and the whole field. Such a catch hasn't been made in the close for years, and the cheering is maddening. 'Pretty cricket,' says the captain, throwing himself on the ground by the deserted wicket with a long breath; he feels that a crisis has passed.

122

But to return to Mr Marshall. The crisis never passed for him. Reams of *Wizards* and *Hotspurs*, volumes of Wisdens and pages of *Boys' Own* all failed to convince him that there was any place on earth for W. G. Grace's confirmed duffer. For Mr Marshall saw himself as nothing more than fodder for the more manly, clear-sighted and privileged members of his school.

At cricket there was never any thought of excusing those unfortunate enough to wear glasses. It was pre-contact lens days and short-sighted boys left their spectacles in their blazers in the pavilion. They stood, when batting, blinded by the sun and enfeebled by cruel nature, peering uncertainly up the pitch in a hopeless attempt to see whence Nemesis was coming. They had to rely heavily on their other senses. Their sense of hearing supplied the thud and thunder of the bowler's cricketing boots, the wicket-keeper's heavy breathing (now coming from a lower angle as he crouched down in readiness) and the disagreeable whistling sound of the ball itself, which indicated that it had been released and was on its way. Their sense of smell supplied the wind-borne unpleasantness of hot flannel, hot sock, hot boy, all of minimal value as directional guides. And their sense of touch told them, sharply and painfully, that the ball had arrived.

And here there was an unfairness. The boys in the first and second elevens, fully sighted and well able to protect themselves, were provided with a contraption called a 'box', a snug and reinforced padded leather compartment worn about the crutch and into which they tucked, I assume, whatever came most easily to hand. It would have been considered a great impertinence for any lesser player to plead for this protection. In the lower echelons, our genitals were expendable.

In Middle Meadow

There was a player in a Sussex village by the name of Percy White. When he gave up umpiring he used to sit and watch from the green wooden seat just by the gate that led into Marshall's orchard. Around about July, he'd get hay fever. His eyes would go red and you could hear him sneeze as far as Frickley Hollow. He was like that when his son, young Len, didn't get a hundred on his fifty-third birthday, which was a pity, because it would have been the first hundred he'd ever got. He was on 98 when the parson from Frickley-by-Weston bowled his full toss. Young Len reckoned it was just as he was going to give it the long handle that he heard Percy sneeze. The whole village heard him sneeze, except, that is, the parson from Frickley-by-Weston, because he was that excited. Young Len said that Percy's sneeze had put him off and that's why he didn't get a hundred. And that's why the parson from Frickley-by-Weston got his only wicket in seven years. . . . That was all back in the forties when, in some parts, village cricket was about the same as it had been for years before the war. It was far removed from the back-street, wall-chalked games in the north country. It was nothing like the carefully manicured colonial backdrop to ever-frosted glasses and cool lawn figures ignoring the cricket just as they ignored the approaching end of the Raj. Yet it was the nearest thing to the county game. For to be found in the village match was the reflection of the Gentleman and the Player. It was the easy preservation of the class distinction of the Long Room. And so village cricket continued to be the beneficiary of the Hambledon Inheritance. Norman Nicholson must have seen that game, the other side of Marshall's orchard:

The Field

Let me first describe the field:
Its size, a double acre; walled
Along the north by a schoolyard,
West by a hedge and orchards; tarred
Wood railings on the east to fence
The grass from the station shunting lines,
That crook like a defensive ditch
Below the ramparts of the Church;
And south, the butter meadows, yellow
As fat and bumpy as a pillow,
Rumpling down the mile or more
That slopes to the wide Cumbrian shore,
With not a brick to lift a ban
Between the eye and the Isle of Man.
A common sort of field you'll say:
You'd find a dozen any day
In any northern town, a sour

Flat landscape shaped with weed and wire,
And nettle clump and ragworth thicket –
But this field is put by for cricket.
Here amongst the grass and plantains
Molehills matter more than mountains,
And generations watch the score
Closer than toss of peace and war.
Here, in matches won and lost,
The town hoards an heroic past,
The legendary bowlers tie
The child's dream in the father's lie.
This is no Wisden pitch; no place
For classic cuts and Newbolt's verse,
But the luck of the league, stiff and stark
With animosity of dark
In-grown village and mining town
When evening smoke-light drizzles down,
And the fist tight in the trouser-pocket,
And the heart turns black for the want of a wicket.

Or knock-out cricket, brisk as a bird,
Twenty overs and league men barred –
Heels in the popping crease, crouch and clout,
And the crowd half-coddling the batsman out.
Over the thorn and elder hedge
The sunlight floods, but leaves a ledge
Of shadow where the old men sit,
Dozing their pipes out. Frays of light
Seam a blue serge suit; gnats swarm,
And swallows dip around the bowler's arm.
Here in a small-town game is seen
The long-linked dance of the village green:
Wishing well and maypole ring,
Mumming and ritual of spring.

The 1940s? It could as easily have been the 1840s, for

there is an almost timeless array of emotions about the greatest game. It is a game of village contrasts wherever it is played. The languid Ranji in wrist-buttoned silk, the broad-belted blacksmith or the huffing doctor with his Emmanuel tie stretched tight about his failing waist. And the jibes and jigs of the lads with all to win.

The Song Of Tilly Tally

O, I say, you Joe,
Throw us the ball!
I've a good mind to go
And leave you all.
I never saw such a bowler
To bowl the ball in a tansy
And clean it with my handkercher
Without saying a word.

That Bill's a foolish fellow;
He has given me a black eye.
He does not know how to handle a bat
Any more than a dog or cat;
He has knock'd down the wicket,
And broke the stumps,
And runs without shoes to save his pumps.

William Blake

They say that cricket began in the southern villages. It was a bruising game played before sandy and brown small-bricked cottages and timbered frames as tough as the legs that bled each game. A hundred years and more ago for Mary Russell Mitford, cricket was for honour and glory and supper and half-a-crown a man:

I doubt if there be any scene in the world

more animating or delightful than a cricket match – I do not mean a set match at Lord's Ground, for money, hard money, between a certain number of gentlemen and players, as they are called – people who make a trade of that noble sport, and degrade it into an affair of bettings, and hedgings and cheatings, it may be, like boxing or horse-racing; nor do I mean a pretty fête in a gentleman's park, where one club of cricketing dandies encounter another such club, and where they show off in a graceful costume to a gay marquee of admiring belles, who condescend so to purchase admiration, and while away a long summer morning in partaking cold collations, conversing occasionally, and seeming to understand the game – the whole being conducted according to ball-room etiquette, so as to be exceedingly dull. No! The cricket that I mean is a real solid old-fashioned match between neighbouring parishes, where each attacks the other for honour and a supper, glory and half-a-crown a man. If there be any gentlemen amongst them, it is well – if not, it is so much the better. Your gentlemen cricketer is in general rather an anomalous character. Elderly gentlemen are obviously good for nothing; and your beaux are, for the most part, hampered and trammelled by dress and habit; the stiff cravat, the pinched-in-waist, the dandy-walk – oh! they will never do for cricket! Now, our country lads, accustomed to the flail or the hammer (your blacksmiths are capital hitters) have the free use of their arms; they know how to move their shoulders; and they can move their feet too – they can run; then they are so much better made, so much more athletic, and yet so much lissomer – to use a Hampshire phrase, which deserves at least to be good English. Here and there, indeed, one meets with an old Etonian, who retains his boyish love for that game which formed so considerable a branch of his education; some even preserve their boyish proficiency, but in general it wears away like the Greek, quite as certainly, and almost as fast; a few years of Oxford, or Cambridge, or the Continent, are sufficient to annihilate both the power and the inclination. No! a village match is the thing – where our highest officer – our conductor (to borrow a musical term) is but a little farmer's second son; where the spectators consist of the retired cricketers, the veterans of the green, the careful mothers, the girls, and all the boys of two parishes, together with a few amateurs, little above them in rank, and not at all in pretension; where laughing and shouting, and the very ecstasy of merriment and good-humour prevail: such a match, in short, as I attended yesterday, at the expense of getting twice wet through, and as I would attend tomorrow, at the certainty of having that ducking doubled.

Now Bill Awker would have laughed out loud at such sights. Bill Awker was known to Hugh de Selincourt, who caught the magic of village cricket during the years between the Great War and the next one. At his public school de Selincourt learned how to play correctly. He knew how to get in line, how to move his feet, when to drop his wrists, and he was very proud of his cap and his carefully washed linen.

He recalled that he might have been the object of much witty good-humoured comment as he stepped carefully to the wicket to face Bill Awker, for the 'him' in the first sentence that follows is de Selincourt:

Bill Awker, a wiry old chap who opened the bowling for a neighbouring village, found him especially amusing. Bill scorned to be dressed up in pretties. He lurched out in huge hob-nailed boots and corduroys to the wicket, took off his collar and tie, put them in the pocket of his jacket, which he removed and handed to the umpire. Then he rolled up his sleeves, fitted his cutty behind his buckled belt, spat on his hands, took the ball from his trouser pocket, stepped two paces back, and crying out, 'Look out for this one, then,' proceded to deal the swiftest lob that skimmed like a frantic little wood gone crazy over the grassy pitch at a petrifying pace, a real authentic daisy-cutter, dead on the wicket. Bill gave his hands an extra rub when he observed my exquisitely accoutred approach to the wicket, and greeted my immediate discomfiture with a horrid shout of laughter. Out came his cutty, out came exuberant puffs. I could never play him then. I am sure I could not play him now. Well, Old Bill has gone – rest his soul! – and many like him. I have not seen such bowling of late years (fortunately for my self-respect) and it is the man or boy not in full cricketing kit who is apt to rouse good-humoured comment now.

The poor lad, but a fine cricketer he became. Of course Awker was not unplayable. And although

Miss Mitford may have been full of impatience with the dandies, her beloved village lads would have been delighted to have given Awker a lesson or two.

A hundred years – and a few more – after Miss Mitford's village, the king was to be crowned in London. A solemn occasion and therefore one for serious action, at least for de Selincourt's Sussex village side. A meeting was called of Annual and General purpose to consider matters not of the new king's state, but of graver and more ancient lore. And what business occupied this concoction of batters, bowlers, keepers and duffers?

The meeting of our cricket club in the library of the village hall bore ample witness to this spirit of derring-do. In Coronation Year – not to have a new coat of paint on the Pavilion! Absurd. Not to have water laid on – preposterous, in Coronation Year! And a small pipe extended to the square (at such trifling cost) so that in the event of a drought (we heard the perpetual rain falling outside and stamped in furious applause) – in the event of a drought (I repeat the word as the dauntless speaker repeated it) the pitch might be watered, the grass kept greener, the turf in smiling, proper condition? There never was such a meeting. When enthusiasm simmered down a little from boiling point to more normal procedure the flame was turned up, relit as from fresh jets, by astute reference to his late Majesty's Playing Fields Funds, and to the 150th anniversary celebration of the great home of all cricket – 'Our own ground, gentlemen, being hardly less ancient; famed in story, though not named in Wisden.'

There never was such a meeting. It was almost funny. It was almost frightening. The staider members were thankful that the whole meeting did not emerge en bloc to the ground, collecting cans of petrol on their jubilant way, apply a match to the tumbledown wooden shack that disgraced the name of pavilion, and while they watched the glad blaze in the dark, damp Spring night, vote vociferously that a new pavilion should arise in stone glory like a Phoenix from the smouldering ashes of old.

The grand meeting before the season's start is the hope of a summer to come. For that dark night the winter dominoes are left in their box and none will hunt for the five-four nor the double six. Instead there'll be talk of averages and who will bowl, and who will write the score and the names for the parish board. But when summer does come, it sometimes affects a modesty that only tempts early farmers to smile, for rain keeps no calendar and respects no fixture card. Edmund Blunden sat and waited patiently for the first sign that rain had wearied:

The summer seems to have fallen into low spirits, and there is nobody about except the rooks and pigeons – we have heard all they have to say – and a crying woodpecker down under the oak at the river. The storm drifts, the cloud-edges are effaced; but the rain patters steadily on the metal roof of the mowing shed, the gutters gurgle, all the trees are grey with the shower. Past the far side of the field a figure with a sack for hood drives his cycle apace, never turning his eyes this way for a

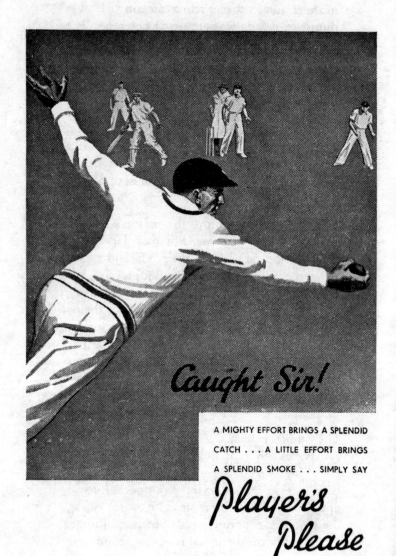

Caught Sir!

A MIGHTY EFFORT BRINGS A SPLENDID CATCH . . . A LITTLE EFFORT BRINGS A SPLENDID SMOKE . . . SIMPLY SAY

Player's Please

moment; and no one from the vicarage steps out to see if there is any prospect of play.

Yet the hours pass, and after all the rain has wearied, and stopped. The smoky-looking day may remain thus, neither better nor worse, and the turf is good. A bicycle is being pushed through the meadow gate by a cricketer in flannels under his macintosh, and one by one they all assemble. An unlocking of padlocks and shifting of benches in the pavilion, a thump of bats and stumps being hauled out of dark corners. The creases are marked, and the offer of a bowling screen rejected. Our boys put catapults back in their jackets and affect to know personally the visitors now arriving, pointing out one or two with awe – that one who hits sixes, and that one with the spectacles who never scores less than seventy. There are not many cricket caps on show, and some of the players are observed to feel safest with braces and ties on.

Sawdust wanted! The fielding side have spread themselves about the soaked ground, and all is otherwise ready – even the two batsmen have gone out to their creases, casting rather unhappy looks on their companions in the pavilion, who sit down in a row and brood. It is odd, this serious game; perhaps it is the greyness of the day that causes it to take this mood.

A New Day

Why does it always rain on the day of the flower show match? Or nearly always. There are times when the foreigner may believe that test cricket is about measuring puddles and getting angry with umpires who hide in the pavilion long after the umbrellas have come down. Edmund Blunden wrote of a gloomy afternoon when summer seemed to have fallen into low spirits. The path to the village pitch was slippery with mud and rain dripped through broad leaf trees. But the rain wearied and stopped. Soon the fieldsmen gathered. There would be play. But first bring the dusty sack from the pavilion's farthest corner, for there must be sawdust in which to duck the soggy and red-staining ball:

> Sawdust! A bucket is being carried forth by the groundsman, whose squat shoulders and beard look like the picture of Hudibras; he

tips out his two little mounds of sawdust, and marches off to his shed, as who should say, 'that is the end of the match for me. That is the match.' The one-armed bowler measures his run, dips the ball into the sawdust, and with three or four sharp steps whizzes it at the opposed batsman; it passes with a wet smack into the gloves of the man behind the stumps. All the fieldsmen attend gravely. This bowler has pace. But no smile.

But the ball won't turn and after a time the batsman lose their reverence and risk sending it over the head of the little man at point; the score is hoisted, and the bowlers are changed. It is mainly that schoolboy who is the cause of this. His score in the book is inspected, it adds up to 18 already. He looks too delicate to perform among these rugged elders, but he is calm enough. At last a large hand and circling arm send him a ball which sails up very much like the one before which he carted over peering faces into the long wet grass; it falls shorter, hits him on the boot. He knows his offence, and the umpire does not let him off; but his innings has gone far enough. There are several batsmen to follow him, and already the total is one which in these games of strong trundlers may serve – 50 up. The boy who has seen to this matter and accepted the punishment for his single error so immediately goes walking away there, with his hands stuck in his green jacket, as if on Robinson Crusoe's island, to the far parts of the field. He seems to have this cricket business in his pocket. When he was questioned just now as he put his pads away 'what the bowling was like', he answered slowly and peacefully, 'The fellow from the lower end turns them a little from the off.'

Such maturity. Yet not every youngster is destined for a great career with the bat. Just as not every flower show match is rained off. Siegfried Sassoon might have been writing about himself when young George Sherston, home among the Kent fruit orchards from his public school, went out to bat for his village, Butley. All was to play for:

When I arrived the Reverend Yalden was dawdling up the pitch in his usual duck-footed progress when crossing from one wicket to another.

'Well young man, you've got to look lively this time,' he observed with intimidating jocosity. But there seemed to be a twinkle of encouragement in Seamark's light blue eyes as I established myself in his shadow.

Dixon played the first three balls carefully. The fourth he smote clean out of the ground. The hit was worth six, but 'three all round and four over' was an immemorial rule at Butley. Unfortunately, he tried to repeat the stroke, and the fifth ball shattered his stumps. In those days there were only five balls to an over. Peter Baitup now rolled up with a wide grin on his fringed face, but it was no grinning moment for me at the bottom end when Sutler gave me 'middle-leg' and I confronted impending disaster from Crump with the sun in my eyes. The first ball (which I lost sight of) missed my wicket by a 'coat of varnish' and travelled swiftly to the boundary for two

138

byes, leaving Mr Yalden with his huge gauntlets above his head in an attitude of aggrieved astonishment. The game was now a tie. Through some obscure psychological process my whole being now became clarified. I remembered Shrewsbury's century and became as bold as brass. There was the enormous auctioneer with the ball in his hand. And there, I, calmly resolved to look lively and defeat his destructive aim. The ball hit my bat and trickled slowly up the pitch. 'Come on!' I shouted, and Peter came gallantly on. Crump was so taken by surprise that we were safe home before he'd picked up the ball. And that was the end of the Flower Show match.

A carefree picture of a young man being for one moment a hero. Later, Sherston went to the Great War and saw a game where the heroes die:

'I see them in foul dug-outs, gnawed by rats,
And in the ruined trenches, lashed with rain,
Dreaming of things they did with balls and bats.'

Far from the horror of those trenches where rain never wearied and never stopped the vile play, the village match continued, an illusion of 'civilization under the sun' and watched knowingly by Gerald Bullett:

Village Cricket

Flowing together by devious channels
From farm and brickyard, forest and dene,
Thirteen men in glittering flannels
Move to their stations out on the green.

Long-limbed Wagoner, stern, unbudging,
Stands like a rock behind the bails.
Dairyman umpire, gravely judging,
Spares no thought for his milking pails.

Bricklayer bowls, a perfect length.
Grocery snicks and sneaks a run.
Law, swiping with all his strength,
Is caught by Chemist at mid-on.

Two to the boundary, a four and a six,
Put the spectators in fear of their lives:
Shepherd the slogger is up to his tricks,
Blithely unwary of weans and wives.

Lord of the manor makes thirty-four.
Parson contributes, smooth and trim,
A cautious twelve to the mounting score:
Leg-before wicket disposes of him.

Patient, dramatic, serious, genial,
From over to over the game goes on,
Weaving a pattern of hardy perennial
Civilization under the sun.

Oh the temptation to believe it true. Is it not part of
the secret wish that things must not change, that
village cricket must be as the long-limbed wagoner,
perhaps not stern, but unbudging like a rock? For the
sight of the village match is reassuring because it is a
dream of Hambledon. In the late 1920s Sir John
Squire dreamed that 'the past could be partly
recovered'. He saw Broadhalfpenny 'now deserted, a
bleak upland with a glorious view and Nyren's Bat
and Ball inn visited by an occasional slumbrous
carter'. And on New Year's Day two sides met where
Silver Billy and Old Nyren had played perhaps a
hundred and fifty years before:

Eight years ago, On New Year's Day, certain Hambledonians (in the old Hambledon tradition they roped in people from all over the country) raised an eleven to play against an eleven raised by me, as a protest against the way in which professional football was nibbling at the cricket season at both ends. The match was 'Hampshire Eskimos' versus 'Invalids' – the Eskimos subsequently turned themselves into a touring club, and long may they flourish with their snow-white caps and blazers adorned by a running red fox.

The old spirit was recovered. The captain of the other side, Mr Whalley-Tooker, had been in the Eton eleven the year I was born. The Master of the local hounds (Major Talbot-Ponsonby) gallantly produced a bye-day for his Hunt. Though international publicity there had been none, several thousands of people turned out, charabancs from Portsmouth, two brass bands, and a vast concourse of riders. It is not surprising that the Bat and Ball was soon at the end of its resources.

There was a matting wicket, and we had arranged that we should play even were there a snowstorm, a deluge, or a fog. We were lucky; there was brilliant sunshine, and a cloudless blue sky, and just as the game began, hounds found (we were assured it wasn't a bagman) in roots, in the westward valley, and careered after him in full sight of us, for several minutes. Some excellent cricket was played, among those distinguishing themselves on the winning side (the visitors won by eleven runs) being a Mr A. D. Peters (whose innings was worthy of Lord's), Mr Howard

Marshall, who had risen from a sick-bed in the expressed hope of hitting a six on Broadhalfpenny on New Year's Day, and actually hit the only six (through the inn window), and Mr (now Sir) Walter Monckton, KC, who was in his old form behind the stumps.

The evening ended at the George in the old Hambledonian way: a large assembly, supper, flowing bowls, song, and even 'The Lost Chord' on a cornet. Some suggested making it an annual event. Had we had foul weather we might have tried it next year. But a repetition of that perfect day, fox and all, was too much to expect; and it was wiser to let it remain a memory undimmed by an anti-climax.

And what of G. D. Martineau's simple lines to ease us gently into an almost idyllic, and therefore dangerously illusionary village scene?

The Village Pitch

They had no Grand Stand or Marquee,
Down by the Quarry Farm:
There was a wealth of leafy tree
Behind the bowler's arm

There were no score-cards to be had,
Cushions for folk to hire;
Only we saw the butcher's lad
Bowl out the village Squire.

Lord's and the Oval truly mean
Zenith of hard-won fame,
But it was just a village green
Mothered and made the game.

Just a village green, but still the scene of hard-won fame. To bowl out the squire! But imagine on that same wicket, in that same hamlet, to bowl out the Australians. In his *Game of the Season* Hugh de Selincourt had the Australians playing Tillingfold. De Selincourt allowed the Australians to win the toss, they batted, they were all out for 39. . . . And then Teddie White came in to bat for the village and found himself surrounded by stern-eyed and green-capped fieldsmen. But Mr Armstrong, for all his time leading his team to victories against the counties and then the MCC, never quite understood that a tight field has never bothered a true agriculturist armed with a hefty bat:

> Teddie White did not go for niceties; he didn't bother about the field; it didn't matter to him where they happened to be placed; his one aim in batting was to put the ball out of their reach, out of the ground, much the safest place. But he had a kind heart, and noticing that fieldsmen were crowded rather nearer to him than they usually were, as Mr Armstrong bowled, he cried out: 'Look out for yourselves then,' as he might have done to careless boys at the village net, and lashed it for four.

And then to the pub to sit there and beam good-naturedly as the game is replayed. Off the back foot, the front, the cut, the slash, the googly that was never so, the yorker, the catch held low. But where is the squire? There is the butcher's boy who bowled him last week. Not there? Perhaps in the garden? No? Ah, of course, there's a private game at the big house in the next village. The house match, an elegant affair. If invited up to play, a fellow might find himself bowling against a man from London. H. D. G. Leveson-Gower laid down the protocol for such a day:

> The cricket itself ought to be of sufficient importance to interest everybody, but not to be allowed to degenerate into an infatuation, and therefore a nuisance to the fair sex. The ground ought not to be too good, for a perfect pitch takes the heart out of the bowling and long scoring can be over-indulged in. All the four totals over 100 and under 200 was A. G. Steel's ideal game, and it's about the best. The games should have local interest, and should if possible bring over one or two cricketers known to the house party.
>
> As for the cricket lunches, most delightful of all Benedick meals, on no account let hospitality spoil them. Champagne lunches are being horribly overdone. Men do not play good cricket on Perrier Jouet, followed by crème de menthe, with two big cigars topping a rich and succulent menu. No, give us some big pies, cold chickens, and fine sirloin of English Beef, and a round of brawn, washed down by good ale and luscious shandygaff. That is all cricketers want, and kings only fare worse.

And so the season slips by and the autumn sweeps its leaves across the boundary's edge. And bat and ball and bails rest in darkened shed. Winter's howl and cruel stare defies tales of deeds told over the snap and clatter of white-spotted dominoes. And then, frost forgotten, the first cut and rake promise a new summer, of old men wondering if it'll be the same; of youngsters, broader in shoulder, longer in gait, waiting to test new skills. Edmund Blunden surely felt all this when he wrote:

The Season Opens

And now where the confident cuckoo takes flight
Over buttercups kindled in millions last night
A labourer leans on the stockyard's low wall
With the hens bothering round him, and dreams bat
   and ball;
Till the meadow is quick with the masters who
   were,
And he hears his own shouts when he first trotted
   there;
Long ago; all gone home now; but here they come
   all!
Surely these are the same, who now bring bat and
   Ball?

Close of Play

At the edge of the field, beneath a broad oak, a sprawled figure rests, back against the brown split bark, eyes half closed. On his lap a book lies open. In the distance the hum of contented voices round a lullaby of names and deeds. A soft wind rustles a page and great names of old bend and arch as if with pride. Far away a stone-faced wall with smudged chalked stumps warms in the same sun. The tree, the wall, the pavilion's door have long played foil and porter to the game of old. The dozing figure sighs and dreams of names and heroes the book still knows. The church's tower chimes the after-hour and flannelled fools at the wicket stand and wait for the white-coated figure to call play.

This Game, they say, was born five hundred years ago and became a man in Hambledon. There, Old Nyren talked of Beldham and Small while some wondered if they'd see their like again. Later others pointed knowingly at Spofforth and Grace. Artists sketched Hendren and Hobbs, Fender, and Bradman. Another war and it was forgotten, as Compton and Hutton and those who followed let us forget the names their fathers had rhymed. And beneath it all the cradle was still rocked. In the village, spring gave way to the first warm days and the rusting roller creaked and cranked over a bed-soft wicket. And small boys who knew no names from pompous past gathered to bowl too fast and play too wide. They became apprenticed to The Greatest Game of All. And others held secret a care that the season, barely started, would be their last:

Ballade of Cricket

The burden of hard hitting; slog away!
Here shall thou make a 'five' and there a 'four',
And then upon thy bat shall lean, and say,
That thou art in for an uncommon score,
Yea, the loud ring applauding thee shall roar,
And thou to rival Thornton shalt aspire;
When lo, the Umpire gives thee 'leg before' –
'This is the end of every man's desire.'
The burden of much bowling, when the stay
Of all thy team is 'collared', swift and slower,
When 'bailers' break not in their wonted way,
And 'yorkers' come not off as here-to-fore;
When length balls shoot no more – ah never
    more!
When all deliveries lose their former fire,
When bats seem broader than the broad
barn- door –
'This is the end of every man's desire.'
The burden of long fielding, when the clay
Clings to thy shoon in sudden shower's
    downpour,

And running still thou stumbles; or the ray
Of blazing sun doth bite and burn thee sore,
And blind thee till, forgetful of thy lore,
Thou dost most mournfully misjudge a 'skyer',
And lose a match the Fates cannot restore –
'This is the end of every man's desire.'

Envoy

Alas, yet liefer on Youth's hither shore
Would I be some poor Player on scant hire,
Than king among the old who play no more –
'THIS is the end of every man's desire.'

Old Andrew Lang wrote that, and wondered. Oh
why do sane men play this game? Why, when foolishness lurks at every elbow to spring out and say boo,
so that everyone might hear and, oh dread, see? Why
have men ever played, when in Hambledon's time
bare fingers were splintered between hard ball and
handle and even now a nose can be crushed as easily as
reputation and esteem? Because it is a fair and
honourable, a manly sport. It must be so, must it not?
But listen to the words of A. G. Steel from the last
century:

> . . . I allude to the betting and bookmaking
> element which from the earliest days has been
> the curse of sport. What is the worst feature
> about horse-riding? To what do English
> lovers of true sport owe the fact that every
> racecourse is the rendezvous of the biggest
> blackguards and knaves in the kingdom? Is it
> not betting, and the pecuniary inducement it
> offers to every kind of dirty, shabby practice?
> The sullying influence has spread to the

CORFU GARRISON CRICKET MATCH, 1863

running-path, and even, if report says true, to the river. Happily there is never the slightest whisper of suspicion against the straightness of our cricket players, and this is entirely owing to the absence of the betting element in connection with the game. It is an unfortunate fact that the tendency of first-class cricket nowadays is to swamp the amateur by the professional. Some of our best county teams are almost wholly composed of the latter class. . . . What has happened in consequence? Cricket – i.e., first-class cricket – is becoming a regular monetary speculation. Thousands upon thousands troop almost daily to see the big matches, flooding the coffers of county or club, which does its very best to spin out the match for the sake of the money. If this continues, our best matches will become nothing better than gate-money contests, to the detriment of the true interests of the game and its lovers.

In earliest times there were great sums to be made, and spent, and new ideas to be formed among the average mongering and money-making. In 1807 the *Morning Herald* noted a game being played for 1,000 guineas and a departure from under-arm bowling:

On Monday, July 20th, the return grand match between a thirteen of All England and twenty-three of Kent, for one thousand guineas, on Bennenden Heath, terminated in favour of Kent by 162 runs. This was reckoned the greatest match by players in Kent for upwards of twenty years. Bets to a large amount depended on both sides. The

151

straight-arm bowling, introduced by John Willes, Esq., was generally practised in the game, and proved a great obstacle against getting runs in comparison to what might have been got by straightforward bowling. This bowling met with great opposition. Mr Willes and his bowling were frequently barred in making a match, and he played sometimes amid much uproar and confusion. Still he would persevere, till the 'ring' closed on the players, the stumps were lawlessly pulled up, and all came to a standstill.

Few batsmen cared for the new bowling, which some say John Willes of Kent learned from his sister. She used to bowl practice balls to him in the barn and because of the voluminous skirts of the day had to bowl a form of round-arm. And so, it is said, over-arm bowling started because of a woman. But of course the fair ladies were not taken too seriously as cricketers, as W. G. Grace observed in 1891:

A new chapter – and a short one – was added to the annals of cricket by the appearance this season of two Elevens of 'Lady Cricketers', who travelled about the country and played exhibition matches. They claimed that they did play, and not burlesque, the game, but interest in their doings did not survive long. Cricket is not a game for women, and although the fair sex occasionally join in a picnic game, they are not constitutionally adapted for the sport. If the lady cricketers expected to popularise the game among women they failed dismally. At all events, they had their day and ceased to be.

'MISS WICKET' (FROM AN OLD PRINT, 1770)

A woman's place is in the tea-hut. Obviously the dears had done enough by bringing about strange bowling. And who could doubt the wisdom of the old cricketers? They were a special breed, you know. They were giants, who hit harder and bowled faster and fielded more furiously than any who came after them:

There were splendid cricketers then, you know,
There were splendid cricketers then;
The littlest drove for a mile or so,

And the tallest drove for ten;
With Lang to bowl and Hankey to play,
Webbe and Walker to score and stay –
And two that I know but may not say –
But we are a pitiful race of clay,
And never will score again.
For all of we,
Whoever we be,
Come short of the giants of old, you see.

E. E. Bowen

But then nothing is the same, nor as good, as the memory saw it. Nothing will be better than that one game when they batted all day and the next, and lost by one ball that suddenly turned. And what of that one moment long forgotten by all others? That brief glory, the straight, anonymous bat while the captain

FIG. 1. THE RIGHT WAY   FIG. 2. THE WRONG WAY
        TO CATCH.   TO CATCH.

stroked the winning runs. Perhaps a catch. Even *the* Catch. For is not a catch the greatest thing after a glorious six? The easy one which drops like a slowly lobbed beach ball may stop the heart. The fast, sharp chance that goes to hand may last longer than the sweetest cover drive. As Alfred Cochrane once wrote, it is the catch that stays in the memory when all others have forgotten:

The Catch

Stupendous scores he never made,
But perished ever with despatch;
No bowling genius he displayed,
But once, in a forgotten match,
He made a catch.

No doubt a timely stroke of luck
Assisted him to do the trick;
He was at cover, and it stuck;
It travelled fairly low and quick –
The kind that stick.

His friends the proud achievement classed
As fortune's most eccentric whim,
And ere a week or two had passed
The memory of the catch grew dim
To all but him.

To all but him, for he relates.
With varying ornament and phrase,
The story to the man who waits
Unwilling in Pavilion ways,
On rainy days.

The catch has grown in splendour now –
He had a dozen yards to run;
It won the match, as all allow,

And in his eyes there blazed the sun,
And how it spun.

Life of old memories is compact,
And happy he for whom with speed
Blossoms a gorgeous tree, where fact
Has planted, in his hour of need,
A mustard seed.

Life of old memories is compact indeed. The past is a great comfort as we mourn heroes and, rarely, those who fell about them. It is the way of the English and so it is with The Game. The code, the Laws, the heroes, the triumphs and oh, the most gallant failures let some stand tall although others scoff and hiss and sigh at the cant. Cricket reigns through the islands. From the cradle of Sussex, Kent, Surrey and Hampshire greens, through the wolds and dales to the slate grey yards and streets, to the river-banked border country. For as Hubert Phillips once told us, an Englishman's crease is 'is castle:

An Englishman's Crease

I've been standin' 'ere at this wicket since
   yesterday, just arter tea;
My tally to date is eleven and the total's an
   'undred an' three;
The crowd 'as been booin' an' bawlin'; it's booed
   and it's bawled itself 'oarse,
But barrackin', bawlin' an' booin' I takes as a
   matter of course.

'Oo am I to be put off my stroke, Mum, becos a
   few 'ooligans boos?
An Englishman's crease is 'is castle: I shall stay
   'ere as long as I choose,

It's not when the wicket's plumb easy that a feller
    can give of 'is best;
It's not 'ittin' out like a blacksmith that wins any
    sort of a Test.
The crowd, they knows nuthink about it; they
    wants us to swipe at the ball;
But the feller 'oo does what the crowd wants, I
    reckon 'e's no use at all,
'Oo am I to be put off my stroke, Mum, becos a
    few 'ooligans boos?
An Englishman's crease is 'is castle, I shall stay
    'ere as long as I choose.

And an Englishman is born to his crease. The truth
must dawn that cricket is a boys' game played by
men. That's why it's so important. As an example,
here is Richard Binns:

A Boys' Game

Does it ever occur, I wonder, to those who
belittle a young boy's efforts in cricket, how
deep-seated these trivial-seeming affections
are and how very much a boys' game cricket
is; how much a boy will sacrifice for it, and
how priceless to him are the lessons of his
cricket apprenticeship, not only in self-
discipline and the formative attributes of character, but as much in the splendid influence of
a single enthusiasm splendidly felt? Are not all
men boys for the greater parts of their lives
because of some flame of keenness in them
which those born old deem irrational? Our
regard for that old bat, a real bat which real
cricketers had handled, was kin to our regard

157

for the great men of the game whom we heard daily about and had not yet seen. In our evening play one boy would suddenly assume an attitude of mock majesty, cocking up his left toe as he grounded his bat in the block-hole, and then loudly announce: 'W.G.!' Another, in whom already some prickings of style could be discerned, would proclaim himself 'F. S.'; another, potentially furious in hitting, would be dubbed 'G. L.' Then would a diminutive bowler, rolling up a torn sleeve as he walked backwards to measure out a run of phenomenal length, retort: 'Right, I'm Spofforth, The Demon. On It!' And as his fearsome delivery came crashing through 'G. L.''s all imperfect defence to smack the tree with a thud that had a finality about it, he would triumphantly add: 'There y' are. Wot did I tell yer? Spofforth. Got yer first ball. Middle stump!' Perhaps I should explain that to us 'On it' was the equivalent of the adult umpire's 'Play'. The grown-up observer amusedly watching this play-acting might too easily miss the truth that lay behind the seeming. I think that lad who for a few moments cloaked himself in the imagined guise of Spofforth donned something more than similitude, and that without it he would not have been able to bring 'G. L.''s innings to so catastrophic a conclusion .

There's none so stubborn as a stubborn cricketer. Nor a dedicated one. But stubbornness and dedication are not always enough. The small boy and the know-ing ancient sit side by side and nod and jibe as padded and tangled legs are made fools of by a small, curving, breaking ball. And when an innings is done, then each will have his say. It was a bowler's wicket that bagged the five, a sturdy stand that husbanded the runs and turned defeat into triumph. But soon there will be another game. The season is all too short and the innings barely begun before the score is entered. Then, as the tins are silent on the old pavilion wall, it is the mason with his stumpy mallet and steel who will record the longest epitaph. But at the close of play the mind will reflect. A good decision? A fair game?

The Pitch at Night

The sunset brings the twilight chill
That steals, all noiseless, on the air.
The wind-freed world is standing still,
The smoothed, worn ground looks strangely bare.

The bowler's run has blurred the crease,
Which glints, a dim and spectral white,
Half sad, half comforting, this peace
That steeled o'er the ground at night.

Steps give a faintly eerie hiss
On less tried turf towards the rough
(Was I too hard on Jone's miss,
Or was I not quite hard enough?)

Here is an ancient, useless pad.
The score-board stares, a square of ink.
Some of this outfield's rather bad . . .
It's colder now; to bed, I think.

G. D. Martineau

And so the season must close. 'It'll be a long winter.' muses one, and another nods and shrugs. It will be so. But yet there is something in the air that calls us to other things and other places. G. D. Martineau trod quietly across the empty field overlooked by spire and early evening lights already flickering on the downs:

It is cold walking over the ground this evening.

Something that was full of warm life and expectation has gone out of the air, and has been replaced by chilly dullness, foreign to the summer season, painful to the subconscious mind.

The icy drops of that short storm had in them none of the tenderness that told merely of a drying wicket and a bowler's day on the morrow. Instead they whipped the pavilion roof with an unfriendly clatter, and the sky showed an unbroken grey to anxious watchers from nearby windows. Now the club flag has been hauled down, and the bare mast stands up like a desolate monument to the dying season.

A solitary match between two scratch elevens remains to be played on the ground, and the bowling screens, accordingly, are left to flap a faint protest, with the last pink of the sunset blessing them.

Far out in the centre can be seen, dimly, the worn patches; scars on the turf, eloquent bowlers' toil, soon to be hidden in the quick growing green. What a season!

So one reflects, going mentally through the tale of hard struggles and their accompanying feats of individual brilliance. It may be that there will be the memory of some personal success, which quickens the pulse and brings back a tingle to the blood. Glad, honest, youthful pride! That was a good day.

Again will come the feel of that late cut, the sublime shudder up the blade that told of an unanswerable boundary; and again one lives the moment of that smart run out: the rash call, the cat-like spring, the lightning return, bails flying . . . a joyous dream that will come back through long years.

The rising wind sends a ripple over the outer grass, and the coldness of it drives one hurriedly down the path past the churchyard – for nearly the last time.

The western sky has turned jet-black, and pin-hole lights are flickering on the downs.

A wonderful year; it is right that it should die so beautifully.

As in life so in death a bat of renown,
Slain by a lorry (three ton);
His innings is over, his bat is laid down:
To the end a poor judge of a run.

George McWilliam

Sources and Acknowledgements

P. 1	Dozing in deckchair's	John Arlott, 'Cricket at Worcester' (1938)
P. 18	Piccadilly Jim	P.G. Wodehouse, *Piccadilly Jim*
P. 19	Chant Royale	H.S. Vere Hodge
P. 21	The first time . . .	Andrew Lang, *Kings of Cricket*
P. 25	There is no other game . . .	E.V. Lucas, *English Leaves*
P. 25	Note that your good cricketer	Mary Russell Mitford, *Our Village*
P. 26	The Victorians so endowed	Neville Cardus, *Cricket*
P. 30	And ye sent them comfits . . .	Rudyard Kipling
P. 32	The Season Opens	Edmund Blunden
P. 36	Denis Compton	R.C. Robertson-Glasgow, *Cricket Prints*
P. 36	Jack Hobbs	John Arlott, *Jack Hobbs*
P. 37	Ranji	Hugh de Selincourt
P. 40	Oldroyd	R.C. Robertson-Glasgow, *Cricket Prints*
P. 41	Cricket	Rev. Reynell Cotton
P. 43	Silver Billy Beldham	John Nyren, *The Cricketers of My Time*
P. 44	John Small	Pierce Egan, *Book of Sports*
P. 45	Bradman	Sir Pelham Warner
P. 46	Percy Fender	Richard Streeton (biography)
P. 47	Silver Billy Beldham	Rev. John Mitford

P. 53	Lord's	Sir Spencer Ponsonby
P. 54	Larwood	R.C. Robertson-Glasgow, *Cricket Prints*
P. 54	Patsy Hendren	R.C. Robertson-Glasgow, *Cricket Prints*
P. 55	I learned the rudiments . . .	W.G. Grace, *Cricketing Reminiscences*
P. 55	I should like to say	W.G. Grace, *Cricketing Reminiscences*
P. 56	Ask any player . . .	W.G. Grace, in *Cricket*, The Badmington Library
P. 57	It is the first long innings . . .	W.G. Grace in, *Cricket*, The Badmington Library
P. 61	Grace at Gloucester	Oscar Lloyd, *West Sussex Gazette* (1948)
P. 61	Lumpy Stevens	John Nyren, *The Cricketers of My Time*
P. 63	David Harris	John Nyren, *The Cricketers of My Time*
P. 69	Piccadilly Jim	P.G. Wodehouse
P. 74	England, Their England	A.G. Macdonnell
P. 78	The Ninth Wicket	A.P. Herbert
P. 81	Lost Ball	E.V. Lucas, *Willow and Leather*
P. 86	Evening Cricket	Charles Dickens, 'Sunday Under Three Heads'

P. 88 Reverend Yalden   Siegried Sassoon,
                              *Memoirs of a Fox-
                              Hunting Man*
P. 89 The Church   Norman Gale, *Cricket
       Cricketant   Songs* (1894)
P. 90 Gravestones   Edmund Blunden
P. 93 At Oxford   The Rev. Pycroft
P. 94 William Grey . . .   Mary Russell Mitford,
                              Our Village
P. 99 If anyone were to   A.G. Steel, Essay
       ask . . .
P. 100 The village   A.G. Steel, Essay
       umpire . . .
P. 102 Australia has always W.G. Grace
       been . . .
P. 104 The writer ventured   A.G. Steel, Essay
       to ask . . .
P. 104 The umpires . . .   Siegfried Sassoon,
                              *Memoirs of a Fox-
                              Hunting Man*
P. 106 Mr Joseph Nicholas,   Bertram Atkey
       Umpire
P. 112 Cricket did have . . . Arthur Marshall, *Boys
                              Will Be Girls*
P. 112 What to do with a   W.G. Grace
       duffer . . .
P. 113 The One Way Boy   R.C. Robertson-
                              Glasgow
P. 116 Crooked meaning   Arthur Marshall, *Boys
       not straight   Will Be Girls*
P. 117 There's music in the Thomas Moult, *Willow
       names . . .   Pattern*
P. 120 'Oh well bowled! . . . Thomas Hughes, *Tom
                              Brown's Schooldays*
P. 123 At cricket there was Arthur Marshall, *Boys
       never . . .   Will Be Girls*

165

P. 126 The Field — Norman Nicholson

P. 128 The Song of Tilly Tally — William Blake, *Songs From an Island in the Moon* (1785)

P. 128 I doubt if there be any . . . — Mary Russell Mitford, *Our Village*

P. 131 Bill Awker, a wiry old chap — Hugh de Selincourt

P. 132 The meeting . . . — Hugh de Selincourt, *The Times, MCC 1777–1937*

P. 133 The summer seems to have . . . — Edmund Blunden, *Cricket Country*

P. 138 When I arrived . . . — Siegfried Sassoon, *Memories of a Fox-Hunting Man*

P. 139 I see them in foul dug-outs . . . — Siegfried Sassoon, *War Poems*

P. 139 Village Cricket — Gerald Bullett, *News From The Village* (1952)

P. 141 Eight years ago . . . — Sir John Squire, *The Times, MCC 1777–1937*

P. 142 The Village Pitch — G.D. Martineau, 'A Score, A score and ten'

P. 143 Teddy White did not go . . . — Hugh de Selincourt, *The Game of the Season*

P. 144 The Cricket Itself . . . — H.D.G. Leveson-Gower

P. 145 The Season Opens — Edmund Blunden

P. 147 Ballade of Cricket — Andrew Lang

P. 148 I allude to the betting — A.G. Steel, Essay

P. 152 A new chapter . . .   W.G. Grace, *Cricketing Reminiscences*

P. 153 They were splendid   E.E. Bowen
cricketers

P. 155 The Catch   Alfred Cochrane, *Collected Verses* (1903)

P. 156 An Englishman's   Hubert Phillips, *News Chronicle* (1951)
Crease

P. 157 A Boy's Game   Richard Binns, *Cricket in Firelight*

P. 159 The Pitch at Night   G.D. Martineau, *The Cricketer*

P. 160 It is cold . . .   G.D. Martineau, 'Salute to Cricket' (*The Cricketer*)

P. 162 As in life   George McWilliam

The Author and the Publishers wish to thank the following for permission to include extracts from copyright works:
John Murray Ltd for *Jack Hobbs* by John Arlott; William Collins Ltd for 'The Season Opens' and *Cricket Country* by Edmund Blunden; Longmans Ltd for *Cricket* by Neville Cardus; Methuen Ltd for *Willow and Leather* by E.V. Lucas; Macmillan Ltd for *England, Their England* by A.G. MacDonnell; Hamish Hamilton for *Boys will be Girls* by Arthur Marshall; Faber & Faber Ltd for *Memoirs of a Fox-Hunting Man* by Siegfried Sassoon; Granada Ltd for *The Game of the Season* by Hugh de Selincourt; Faber & Faber Ltd for *Percy Fender* by Richard Streeton; Harrap Ltd for *Bradman* by Sir Pelhan Warner; A.P. Watt Ltd and the Estate of P.G. Wodehouse for *Piccadilly Jim* by P.G. Wodehouse.

168

Reading List

Not a bibliography, but a short reading list from the author's shelves for those who would find themselves in deckchair's gentle curve and occasionally dreaming about if not watching the cricket . . . (with apologies to Mr Arlott)

History of Cricket, Eric Parker, Seeley Service & Co.
English Cricket, Christopher Brookes, Weidenfeld & Nicolson
The Game of the Season, Hugh de Selincourt, Rupert Hart-Davis
The Cricket Match, Hugh de Selincourt, Rupert Hart-Davis
Denis Compton, Ian Peebles, Macmillan
The Day's Play, A.A. Milne, Methuen
Teddy Lester: Captain of Cricket, John Finnemore, W & R Chambers
WG, W.G. Grace, James Bowden
The English Game, Gerald Brodribb, Hollis & Carter
Summer Days, Edited by Michael Meyer, Methuen
Benny Green's Cricket Archive, Pavilion
England: an Anthology, Macmillan
The Duke Who Was Cricket, John Marshall, Frederick Muller
Quilt Winders & Pod Shavers, Hugh Barty-King, MacDonald & Janes
Cricket's Unholy Trinity, David Foot, Stanley Paul
Cricket Prints, R.C. Robertson-Glasgow, T. Werner Laurie
Penguin Cricketer's Companion, Ed. Alan Ross
Wisden Book of Cricket Quotations, Ed. David Lemon, Queen Anne Press
MCC 1777–1937, Times Publishing
Cricket, Neville Cardus, Longmans

Cricket All the Year, Neville Cardus, Collins
The Essential Neville Cardus, Jonathan Cape
The Way to Lord's, Ed. Marcus Williams, Willow
Middle Ages of Cricket, Ed. John Arlott, Christopher Johnson
Cricket Country, Edmund Blunden, Collins
Archie Jackson, David Frith, Pavilion
English Leaves, E.V. Lucas, Methuen
Jack Hobbs, John Arlott, John Murray
Between Wickets, Ray Robinson, Collins
Lord's, Sir Pelham Warner, Geo. Harrap
The Hambledon Men, Ed. E.V. Lucas, Clarendon Press
Cricketers of the Veld, Louis Duffus, Samson Low, Marston
Cricket Verse, Ed. Gerald Brodribb, Rupert Hart-Davis
The Golden Age of Cricket, David Frith, Omega
Women's Test Cricket, Joan L. Hawes, The Book Guild
Australian Cricket, Jack Pollard, Angus & Robertson
Gentlemen and Players, Michael Marshall, Grafton
Good Company, Ed. E.V. Lucas, Methuen
A History of Cricket, H.A. Altham
Principles of Scientific Batting, Rev. J. Pycroft (1835)
The Cricket Field, Rev. J. Pycroft, (1851)
Felix on the Bat, B. Wanostrocht (1845)
The Cricketer's Manual, Charles Box (1848)
The Theory & Practice of Cricket, Charles Box (1867)
The English Game of Cricket, Charles Box (1877)
Guide to Cricketers, F. Lillywhite (1849)
Echoes From Old Cricket Fields, F. Gale (1871)
Old Cricket and Cricketers, Bishop Montogomery
Cricket as Now Played, Frederick D'Arros Planche, Ward Lock (1877)
Kings of Cricket, Richard Daft, Arrowsmith (1893)